Party of Twelve:
THE AFTERLIFE
INTERVIEWS

D1247701

BARBARA With

PARTY OF TWELVE:
The Afterlife Interviews

With, Barbara
Party of Twelve: The Afterlife Interviews
ISBN: 0-9677458-0-2
Library of Congress Control Number:
200117250

Printed in the United States of America.

www.barbarawith.com
madisland@barbarawith.com

Dedicated to Elton John

Table of Contents

ACKNOWLEDGMENTS

Christina Arneson: *Conceptualization and Motivation, without whom this book would not exist*

Barbara Daughter, Judy Kreag, Dorothy Moga: *Editorialization*

Teresa McMillian, Lily Phelps: *Inspiration*

Gary With: *Solidification*

The Party: *Manifestation*

One night when I was five years old, my grandmother appeared before me. The only trouble was, she was dead. I remembered seeing her coffin lowered into a large hole in the ground some months before, but still, seeing her there that night at the foot of my bed, glowing in the dark, I was surprisingly calm. She told me to tell Mama that her watch was under the chair in the back of her bedroom, and that she and Grandpa were mighty happy, dancing away in heaven.

When I told my mama the next morning, she went immediately to the chair and sure enough, there was the watch that she had misplaced since, oddly enough, the funeral.

Ever after, whenever one of Mama's friends or family needed to contact a dead relative, she'd bring them to me. We'd sit at the kitchen table and over a cup of tea, we'd just talk. As soon as the person said the name of their dead relative, that relative would appear to me, like a hologram, or a memory of a shadow of their presence. I could hear their voice, and converse with them, just like I was talking to a living person. I became the conduit, the interpreter, as if I spoke a special language. It always amazed me that no one else could see the dead people. They were plain as day to me.

When I was ten, I told some kids in my catechism class about Grandma. Father Butler dragged me into his office, where he delivered a fierce lecture on the evils of talking to the dead. He said I was wandering into a realm of the devil and insisted there was a hidden force just waiting to overtake me that would trap me forever in some kind of hell on Earth. I'd become haunted, possessed, and then I'd need an exorcist to remove the wayward spirit.

It was an interesting spin, but it didn't feel right. Grandma wasn't evil, and people were happy and more at peace after they talked to their dead loved ones. The dead people were always very happy that someone was taking them seriously. They weren't really dead anyway. They didn't have physical bodies anymore, no, but they hadn't really gone anywhere either. Anyway, according to Einstein, there's nowhere to go.

I'm not sure I believe in evil. Just because I've never met an evil spirit doesn't mean there aren't any. But I've found that life in spirit isn't much different than life on Earth. In both places, there are forces that can hurt you if you're unprepared. Friends fail us. People get ripped off. Why would it be any scarier in spirit than it is just walking around the streets of America at night?

When I became an adult, the dead people began asking for my help. Dead friends, family members, even people in comas and advanced stages of Alzheimer's would ask to get a message to a loved one, just like how Grandma needed to let Mama know where her watch was. Dead people were such a part of the fabric of my life, I took them for granted. Every message I delivered to the living was to someone who believed in the Afterlife and said they'd felt the presence of their loved one around them anyway, trying to communicate.

Yes, I know, I just sound nutty. Trust me, it's exceptionally nutty. Except, every time I look past the nuttiness and help the dead person with their request, a wonderful thing happens, for their loved one, and, it appears, for the dead person as well. However nutty the means are, the ends bring with them a quiet peace, for everyone involved.

One afternoon, shortly after the funeral of my beloved friend Morton, an angel appeared before me. This was new. He was very large, and had those white, over-sized wings that filled my small rented room. He said he'd come to tell me that soon I'd be asked to deliver a very special message. He made it sound like I was getting drafted into some heavenly mission. What else could I do but nod and agree?

Shortly after his visit, an entire group of angels appeared. They said they had some important information for the world, and they'd heard I might be willing to take some dictation. I agreed to help them, and wrote a book for them with two other women, Teresa McMillian and Kimberly Phelps, "Diaries of a Psychic Sorority: Talking With The Angels." Made me think, angels really have a lot to say.

One late July day, the angels called an emergency meeting. They seemed anxious to tell me something, and made it sound extremely important that I get this information out as quickly as I could. They were overjoyed and said that there was an opportunity for world peace to break out in exactly one year.

I was confused. Hearing this made me nervous. They'd never made a prediction like this before, ever. It seemed like too short a time, in this turbulent world, for even the entire heavenly host to bring peace to every part of the globe in only one year. Someone would have to have a really big influence and be a really great planner to pull this off.

Soon after, out of the blue, I received a phone call from one Tina Spokane, a New York literary agent who had a magazine interested in buying an afterlife interview with Princess Di to run on the anniversary of her tragic death. Tina knew of "Diaries" and thought I would be the perfect writer for the assignment. "Princess Di Speaks From Beyond the Grave." Sounded like something right up my alley. The only problem was, the newspaper that wanted the interview was a tabloid.

Red flags went up all over the place. I didn't know how I felt about talking to Princess Di and then selling it to the tabloids. Would I ruin my reputation as a writer by publishing something in the tabloids? My thought was, which reputation is that? That I talk to dead people and angels?

I examined at length my intentions for doing the piece and how I felt about my work sandwiched between stories about the Clinton sex scandals. I came to the decision that as long as I knew the truth, and there was an interest, then there would be no harm in at least asking Diana what she thought about it.

The next morning, in my basement office in Minneapolis, I sat down at the computer for forty-five minutes and let Diana speak through me. I typed fast and furiously, printed off a copy, tucked it in my beach bag and headed to the lake to swim and edit.

Sitting at a picnic table at what I affectionately call the Third World Beach, I began to read what I had written. I started to cry. At first it was just plain touching, reading about her children, and Dodi. Then I cried harder when she got to the part about what happened at the crash. I wept as I realized, well, I really had spoken to Diana. By the time I was halfway through, I was sobbing into my beach towel.

What was so striking in the interview with Di was her voice. As I read it, I could hear her speaking. Her whole persona was exactly how I'd imagined she'd been in real life. She said she was referred to me by the angels.

Such an honor! She also had a special message for her dear friend Elton. But it was her message for world peace that struck me as the most brilliant part.

I managed to collect myself, but I never did go swimming. I sat and stared out over the lake, absorbing what just happened. Here was a message from Diana, from beyond the grave, inspiring people to make peace in their lives. It might go into a tabloid with a circulation of what? Eight million? Twelve million? Forty-three million?

All the people that read the tabloids would want to know these things about her, that she's fine and still here with us, working mostly with her kids. It dawned on me that the people who read the tabloids are the same ones who put flowers in front of the palace, the ordinary people who loved her for just who she was.

If twelve million people read this and believe it, how many of those people could she inspire to pick up their power and commit to making peace on all levels of their lives? What kind of influence would this have on the world peace predictions the angels delivered in my living room?

Sitting there that afternoon on the picnic bench at the Third World Beach with Diana, I turned to her and said, "It's brilliant."

She said, "Yes, I know, but we are not in charge here."

Thank God we are not in charge. Because I could not think up a plan that brilliant no matter how much you paid me.

The next week, I flew to New York to meet with Fannie, the representative from the British tabloids. She only could "stay a short time" and had "other important appointments," but still managed to spend five hours with us. We picked a restaurant that was "coincidentally" only one block from the St. Regis Hotel, where the reporter swore Elton John began writing "Candle In The Wind."

We parted ways with Fannie that night and never heard from her again. Apparently, there wasn't enough dirt about Prince Charles and the royal kids to interest the tabloids. It didn't matter. Out of my conversation with Diana came the curiosity to see what other famous dead people had to say. Over turkey burgers and margaritas at a restaurant on the Hudson, Tina and I mapped out a plan to talk to eleven more famous dead people who might have something timely and inspiring to say to the world.

We started throwing out names: Ghandi, Mother Teresa, Mussolini, Curt Cobain, Elvis, Joan of Arc, Einsenhower, Jon Benet Ramsey, Abraham Lincoln, Harriet Tubman, John Lennon. How would I ever know who to pick out of such a fascinating array of names? I wanted to know everything about every one of them.

When one of us threw out a name, I would go to that person and ask them if I could do an interview with them, just like any reporter might approach a celebrity. Each one told why he or she didn't want to speak. Ghandi said he'd said it all in his life, as did Mother Teresa. Jon Benet and Curt Cobain said they didn't want to talk yet, for fear of incriminating people they loved. John Lennon wanted to sit this one out, as he shows up everywhere already. Mussolini was indifferent, Einsenhower was busy and Elvis said his experiments with materialization were getting him in too much trouble as it was.

The ones who did want to speak said so decidedly up front and then just waited. It didn't take me long to figure out, it wasn't up to me to decide who would talk. As it turned out, they picked us.

The second person was Nicole Brown Simpson. We interviewed her in Tina's Broadway office the next afternoon. I asked myself if Nicole would hold up in the company of Einstein and Hitler. After reading the transcript, I say absolutely. We don't know how time will hold her memory, but certainly the O.J. trial was one of the most riveting, button-pushing events of the 90s. She deserves to be remembered.

Einstein was very familiar. I think he's been hanging around me a long time. In fact, he all but admitted he was in on "Diaries." He was excited about the idea of being able to talk through me, and was quite a rascal, as I hear he had been while a human on Earth.

The Party of Twelve didn't waste time making it clear that this was not our idea. They'd apparently been cooking this project up for quite some time. They only needed someone wacky enough to believe them, but sane enough to take them seriously. That would be me.

These interviews were conducted between August 16 and September 17, 1998, one month and one day from conception to final interview. Since that time, I've not been sure of what direction to take to get them out into the world. The angels kept telling me not to worry, that there's a bigger plan in play than I could ever imagine.

Shortly after completion of the original twelve interviews, Tina and I had a falling out. So much for world peace. I knew each of us was being stubborn and self-centered, but I was in no hurry to make up with her.

On July 16, 1999, my fifth wedding anniversary, the Kennedy family was hit with yet another tragedy when John Kennedy Jr.'s plane disappeared on his way to Martha's Vineyard. Before his body was found, he appeared to me with his mother and father, and asked if I would allow him speak through me. Jacqueline informed me that he was supposed to write the introduction for their book.

Out of the sadness of yet another Kennedy trauma came the realization of the joy he felt being with his mother and father again. During this time, my vision felt like a split screen: on one hand, I hated seeing the news clips of the family suffering through this agonizing ordeal, and on the other, I loved witnessing JFK, Jackie and John John catching up on old times.

A day after he disappeared, the phone rang. It was Tina. She said she, too, had been visited by John Jr. Apparently he told her that she was supposed to make sure I allowed him to write the introduction. In the gravity of the situation, Tina and I forgave each other for things we had long since forgotten.

It took several months to coordinate the project. Finally, on December 22, 1999, John Kennedy Jr. spoke to us, in a room in a Long Island bed and breakfast. He was anxious to talk, but confused and unaccustomed to working in this way. The session ended shortly after he started. When I asked what was wrong, he said he needed to do more research.

Exactly one month later, on a snowy evening in a Madison hotel room in the shadow of the Wisconsin state capitol building, John delivered his introduction. Clearly he had done his homework, as his words flowed out of me, pre-edited and well-chosen, providing us with the final explanation of what happened that fateful night of his crash, and how the Party of Twelve came together in the Afterlife to facilitate this amazing project.

Is "Party of Twelve: The Afterlife Interviews" nonfiction? Is this really John Jr., Freud and Einstein talking? How can we be sure it's not spirits disguising themselves as these venerable people, or that I'm not just making the whole thing up?

Am I just making the whole thing up? Am I really just a nut case? Alrighty then, if I am a wacko, I'm a hell of a writer.

If that's the case, can we just call it fiction?

I myself believe I spoke with these dead people and that they're really who they say they are. I've talked to dead people all my life and been visited by hierarchies of angels. But more than that, I know these interviews only took one month to write. I know I have a tape recording of me and Tina on the floor of her bathroom on the Upper West Side of Manhattan during a Sunday afternoon thunderstorm with candles lit. Eyes closed, words flowing from my mouth, I believed Albert Einstein was talking through me. And I know what I feel inside me when I listen back on those words or read his chapter.

If you find yourself uneasy with that, please feel free to think I just made the whole thing up. It makes no never mind to me.

Either way, like Diana said, it's brilliant. But then again, I am not in charge.

Barbara With

INTRODUCTION: John Kennedy Jr.

November 25, 1961 – July 16, 1999

"Death"

From the moment of my birth, my life was captured and broadcast on international newsreels. Being so young at the time of my father's death, I had no real recall of saluting his passing, except from what I'd seen in those newsreels. Memories of my early life came from these celluloid moments, frozen in time, that were a part of the history of this great country. That little kid standing at his father's grave was as much a stranger to me as he was to anyone else. And as odd as this might sound, just like the rest of the world, I took him as my own.

When I was older, I saw the Zapruder tape. Watching my father's last day, last moments on the planet, over and over I asked myself unanswerable questions: Did he know these were his last moments? How did he feel waking up to his last day on Earth? Could one decision made differently that morning have changed the entire course of history? There were no answers to these lifelong questions.

I came to believe I'd wake up the morning of my death and know it. But I didn't. My last day on Earth was an ordinary day. Sure, you might wonder if John Kennedy Jr. ever had an "ordinary" day in his life. But even the most powerful, affluent and influential people have ordinary days in relation to what's important to them and their inner circles. Cutting through all demographics, economics, moral and ethical values comes death, the great equalizer.

When I got to the plane that afternoon to do the flight check, I thought, "What if this is my last flight?" But I almost always thought that during flight check, so even that was not extraordinary.

I'd picked up the weather report off the Internet shortly before I left for the airport. It called for winds at 10 knots, visibility six miles, and clear skies. It seemed like an ordinary weather report.

With Carolyn and Lauren strapped in, as we started down the runway, I can honestly say I had no indication that this was the last flight of my human life. We took off into a clear summer evening. Climbing into the altitudes, Carolyn and Lauren discussed the wedding presents they had gotten Rory.

Within seconds, the plane was surrounded by a thick haze. I could hardly see the horizon, and any lights from land were swallowed up in the mist.

Looking back, I see that the moment the haze enveloped us was the beginning realization of my death. An extraordinary fear came over me, like electricity surging through my body. I suppressed this fear the best I could. As the son of John F. Kennedy, I can't begin to tell you what was expected of me in life. Suppressing fear was a survival technique I learned in childhood.

The president's son in me wanted to live up to his father's legacy. The ordinary husband in me wanted to keep my family safe from harm. The macho guy wanted to rise to the challenge and become an ace, able to fly safely through any weather.

Frankly, the crash took place so quickly that no one knew what was happening. I struggled a bit with the controls, but never really knew how out of control I was. Barely enough time to get dizzy, every second was eternity as some deeper part of me knew where we were headed.

The impact was intense, and lightening-fast. At first, there was no difference between being alive and being dead. When the plane hit the water, our consciousness continued on seamlessly without a great deal of turmoil. The only difference was that moments before the crash, there had been an intense whistling around the windows. Suddenly, everything was dead silent.

We didn't realize we had died. In fact, it took us awhile to really know what was going on. We thought we were still in the plane flying through the haze. Nothing seemingly changed, but, in retrospect, everything had, in an instant and we knew it.

For a little while, we speculated about this odd sensation. Since we weren't aware of the crash, we weren't carrying with us some dastardly human memory of a violent end.

Suddenly, I heard my father's voice say, "Nice flying, ace." I whipped around to see him sitting there in the back of the Piper, the same age as when he died, looking fit and rested. I was shocked, elated and completely confused, all at the same time. This felt like waking up in a luscious, lucid dream.

The mists parted, and an island airstrip appeared below us. At first I thought it was Martha's Vineyard, but as we made the approach, I noted a tropical climate below me. My father's hand rested on my shoulder as I landed the plane.

As we taxied to a stop, as if out of some dream sequence my mother appeared on the edge of the tarmac on this island paradise. She was also the age she'd been when Dad died, and more beautiful than ever. With my father smiling behind me and my mother waiting to embrace me, the joy was indescribable.

The elation, the comfort, the love and sense of family was overwhelming. At some point, I recall thinking of everyone we'd left behind, but oddly, I didn't miss them, as if we were on vacation in another part of the world, apart from them but not without them in our hearts. And somewhere inside, I knew they were being comforted by the knowledge of this moment, this reunion with my mother and father.

On seeing my mother again, I finally realized that Death had crept up from behind and gently taken me, in an ordinary way. By the time I figured it out, I was already enveloped in the joy of the Afterlife. The reality of this precious joy was much more powerful than the ideas I'd contemplated when I was on Earth. This was not like thinking about the possibilities of a joyful Afterlife, it was a complete experience entailing all my deepest emotions, farthest-reaching thoughts and, even though I didn't yet understand this part, every molecule of my entire body.

Standing there with my mother and father in that paradise was truly ecstasy. They led us to a great hall where family members who'd died before us were gathered to greet us. Some of them I'd known on Earth, and some I'd only heard stories of and seen in pictures. Here was a great celebration with plenty of time to catch up.

This has always been our family: banding together in times of change. Yes, dying was intense, but still, it was going home.

After meeting with the family, and a short time of rest, I was asked by my parents to attend an editorial meeting. I'd never imagined that after death you might be given editorial assignments. Would the joy never end?

Truthfully? I was a little apprehensive that my mother and father were working on a "project" in the Afterlife. I could tell my mother was trying to prepare me for something. She'd used this same tone when she'd first told me about Ari, reiterating that what she was about to say might take some time for me to grasp. I prepared myself to listen as she encouraged me to adopt my most detached journalist's POV, knowing, of course, that this would pique my interest.

In an instant we were standing at the door of what appeared to be an old jury room. The architecture was from New York City, circa the late 1940s. Etched in the glass in the door was a picture of the Empire State building.

Mother gently opened the door and led me in. Dad followed. A long jury table surrounded by twelve chairs filled the room. Seated in the chairs were various people, some of whom I recognized. Near the head of the table was an empty chair that I assumed was for me. Mother and Dad took their seats in the middle of the table across from each other.

As I looked at the faces, one by one, I understood what my mother had been preparing me for. Sitting at this table were ten of the most influential people from the 20th century, besides my mother and father, of course. My mind simply could not fathom the range of cultural and spiritual knowledge represented by this party.

At the same moment, I realized my life as John F. Kennedy Jr. had prepared me for such a meeting. All throughout my life I sat at the tables of some of the powerful people in the world. I mean, how many kids have one of the largest international airports in the world named after their father? Sitting here was as right as rain. My father proceeded to introduce me.

At the head of the table sat a man who needed no introduction. Albert Einstein grinned like an excited kid happy to see me. I was star-struck, for if there was any one person in history who I'd wanted to meet, it was this amazing man. Here he was, giggling as I shook his hand. I noticed he was young and vital, about the age when he discovered the theory of relativity.

Next to him sat a woman I didn't recognize at first. A beautiful brunette in her mid-thirties, I was shocked when dad said, "John, met Norma Jean Baker." This was not the blonde bombshell she had depicted as Marilyn Monroe. Here was a strong, intelligent woman with a gleam in her eye, and every bit as radiate as Marilyn ever was. I glanced for a moment at my mother, who was smiling and shaking her head.

Sitting beside her was a woman I had written about several times, Nicole Brown Simpson, looking much like she did shortly before her death. My heart grabbed my throat as I saw the sadness in her eyes yet, even in Afterlife. I instantly remembered that long trial, and her children left behind with their father.

Dad was seated next, and beside him sat a man who was clearly European, dressed in a suit straight out of the '30s. Sigmund Freud was young and vital, and like Albert, seemed anxious to get down to business.

Beside Sigmund was a young man of about thirteen. Strong and healthy, he leapt up to meet me. As he stood eagerly pumping my hand, my mother said, "Honey, meet Ryan White." Tears welled up in my eyes seeing him healthy, happy and strong. I had followed his story closely, as AIDS has been an important issue for me. Ryan smiled and gave me two thumbs up.

Seated at the end of the table was a dark figure, ominous and mournful. A pain shot through me when he looked up into my eyes. He'd obviously lived a tumultuous life. Small and frail, he was preoccupied, as if his attention was still focused on something from his life on Earth. Albert introduced him, simply as "my friend Adolph."

A chill ran down me. Adolph Hitler! How could this be? He was not supposed to be in this paradise. I looked again at my mother, who only said, "Everything will be made clear in good time, John."

Next was a handsome young man dressed in a flamboyant coat of iridescent colors. He introduced himself as Gianni Versace and said, "I'd always wanted to meet you on Earth, but truly, it is much better late than never." I smiled and told him I had recently purchased some Versace shoes that I was sorry I'd never get a chance to wear. He laughed heartily and pointed to my feet. There they were! Very cool...

I instantly recognized Anwar al-Sadat. Arab-Israeli politics was a study of mine, and he was something of a hero. Sitting at the table dressed as he had been the day he died, regaled in his military attire was a gentle man of deep insight and quiet grace. As I shook his hand, I looked forward to talking to him one on one.

Mother sat beside Mr. Sadat, and to her right was a man dressed in simple attire that appeared to be from early Roman times. His robe radiated in hues of gold and yellow. In fact, he appeared to be glowing from inside out. When he looked at me, his blue eyes shone with pure compassion. His smile was gentle and deep, and as I took his hand, an energy of peace shot into me that surpassed all my understanding.

"John, this is Jesus of Nazareth," my mother said

quietly, and the impact of this truth rendered me speechless. Jesus laughed, took his hand away and hugged me with such love I began to weep. As he pulled back, he tousled my hair as if I was a small child, and indeed, in that moment I felt childlike and innocent and pure. It was said that just a touch from this teacher was enough to evoke healing from the suffering of an earthly existence. As I stood before him, I knew that was the truth.

The final member of the party, Diana Spencer, Princess of Wales was radiant. She rose from her seat at the table and held out both her hands, which I took between mine. Even though we hadn't been close friends in life, I'd met her on several occasions. What struck me then was her genuine discomfort in being an icon. She longed to be considered an ordinary woman. I recall wishing I could have helped her, or told her how I coped with those challenges. But we never talked of such things in life. Here in the Afterlife, her ordinary presence was breathtaking, and the light shining from within her was stunning. I felt I already knew her.

Diana turned and pulled out the empty chair situated between her and Albert. I took my place, excitedly wondering what this odd collection of souls was up to. Why were they gathered in this jury room, but more importantly, what did they want from me? Albert rose, cleared his throat and began to tell their story.

* * * * * * * * * * *

Upon his death, Albert arrived in the Afterlife in need of rest. The idea of evil haunted him. He took long walks alone, concerned about the world he had left behind. How would these powerful revelations of his about the nature of matter affect the future of humanity? With the atom bomb a reality, had he just unwittingly contributed to the demise of the entire planet? What if he was indeed responsible for supplying the world with a suicidal weapon of mass destruction? Would that make him evil?

He persisted in his investigations into the nature of reality. The Afterlife seemed to have a different set of natural laws. Here, there appeared to be only love, and everyone was clairvoyant. When someone needed privacy, everyone simply knew to respectfully turn the other direction. Everyone was innocent, and those who had chosen hellish actions on Earth were experiencing the repercussions of those hellish choices. But no one judged anyone else, for everyone had their hands full dealing with their own karma.

Manifestation of matter was almost instantaneous. Albert would think about being back on Long Island in his house by the ocean, and in a split second, he'd be experiencing the physical reality of that desire. Many mysteries that eluded him in life, such as time travel, and dematerialization, were revealed and experienced easily here. But an entirely new set of questions and mysteries arose before him as he explored the Afterlife, inside and out. His search for answers continued.

Souls were organized by type into study groups to continue pursuing the growth and evolution of the human spirit. Albert was drawn to those groups working towards global unity and worldwide peace. People from all walks of human life were gathering together in the Afterlife to learn how to influence the planet they'd just left behind. The question was, how, from this place of

Spirit, could communication take place with those still in human bodies? Parents wanted to reach back to their children who remained alive. Albert wanted to tell the world about the missing link in his formulas. The scientist in him, coupled with his deep sense of responsibility, drove him to develop a method to make contact, through dreams, imagination and extrasensory perception. He delighted in showing up in the dreams of the masses.

Albert met often with the many who had lost their lives in the Holocaust. They seemed to move as a force of compassion. Because of their intense suffering together, they were bonded in a way that even they didn't quite understand. Together they explored the meaning of their participation in one of the most devastating and evil periods on Earth.

Evil seemed to fascinate and confound Albert. How could a force of such sweeping devastation and complete absence of empathy and compassion originate from such a divine infrastructure? And more importantly, why? These questions haunted him.

In the form of an answer, one afternoon he unexpectedly found himself standing before a jury room door. Etched in the glass was the Empire State Building, one of his favorite haunts from life on Earth. He chuckled over this New York City depiction of a world on trial. Opening the door revealed three figures huddled at the far end of a long, twelve-person jury table.

One man, facing the door, was intently listening to a second man, who was hunched over in a chair with his back to the door, speaking under his breath. Facing them both stood a third man whose hands, which appeared to be glowing, rested on the shoulders of the dark sloughed figure. Albert could clearly see that the discussion was extremely grave. The mysterious, huddled figure was relating a story of deep agony, and the glowing hands returned only love and forgiveness.

Albert approached the men cautiously. He at first recognized Sigmund Freud. Oh, he had not seen him since Berlin! As their eyes silently met, both turned back to the pathetic figure bent over himself in the chair.

Darkness clung to his skin like soot. His cheeks were drawn and tight around the bones of his face. The air around him smelled of agony.

Then Albert realized: he was watching Adolph Hitler being attended to by Jesus.

Adolph was truly in a living hell. But not the classical sense of *going to* hell. Hell was *coming out* of him, from his deepest insides, burning away every second with agonizing, torturous guilt and unbearable responsibility for what he had done.

He was plagued by questions about his life as well. Why did he do it? What was the purpose? And how long would he suffer in the Afterlife for the crimes he had committed? Why was he even conscious? Why hadn't he just turned to blackness on his death, not fit to be alive?

For every question, Jesus had an answer. Albert was fascinated, amazed, confounded and inspired, all at once. The display of pure compassion was breathtaking. To every sin, every grotesque description of some horrid act of the Holocaust, Jesus responded only in love, forgiveness, compassion, truth. Albert was, for the first time in a long time, speechless.

As they talked, Sigmund took meticulous notes. Soon Albert joined into the discussion and the focus turned gently from Adolph's hell to the world they had left, and the new world they were living in. Einstein expounded on his passion to communicate what they were learning in Afterlife to those they'd left behind. The four talked for what seemed like days. Sigmund wrote like a madman the entire time.

The others soon begun to join them. Norma Jean and John F. Kennedy arrived together. Discussions broadened to include sexuality, feminism, politics and intrigue. Next came Ryan White and Anwar al-Sadat, bringing the focus to the Middle East conflicts, AIDS and peacemaking. Nicole Brown Simpson and Jackie Onassis brought up the topics of domestic abuse, race relations, publishing and power. Gianni Versace arrived insisting on examining culture and its deviations from the center. As the party of twelve grew and expanded their explorations, ideas flowed from one person to the next, and the chapters formed.

By the time Diana Spencer showed up at the door, and the last chair was filled, they had compiled enough information to publish an entire book that covered almost every facet of modern culture. Distilled from all of their experiences while on Earth, their message of compassion, love, forgiveness and truth, broadcast towards human existence, might possibly change the course of human events from destruction to resurrection. If they could communicate "what we know now" to the struggling world, could they really make a difference in the course of human evolution?

Not all party members agreed on the answer to that question. But each and every one felt it was worth a try. This work of peace, originating in Afterlife, fulfilled

Albert's desire to reach back and articulate the one piece that was missing from all his scientific jargon. Here was the answer to preventing his discoveries of relativity from contributing to the destruction of the planet: re-program the infrastructure of the human being from one feeding off fear, to one fueled by honor and love. For in a love-based culture, there would be no need for weapons.

Albert and the party began dissecting the possibilities of how to communicate their information to someone still living on the Earth. Diana had an excellent idea for reaching the millions of people who were interested in reading about her. All that was needed was a living human who was crazy enough to put their words to paper, just as they said them, but sane enough to take their presence seriously. Perhaps a reporter of sorts, or a priest.

Like a prayer answered, an angel referred the party to Barbara, a young woman who had already been in their service. Here was the trust they needed. Barbara agreed to interview Diana. There was the willingness to be wacky. It was perfect.

So began the communication from the Afterlife of knowledge, compassion, truth and inspiration. Like ham radio operators, each member of the party took a turn in sending his or her message through Barbara. For Albert, the process itself was the miracle, an achievement of monumental proportion in the continuing evolution of science and spirit.

* * * * * * * * * * *

Albert finished his story and took his seat. The room was silent. Mother was right, I would need some time to digest all this information. Albert's retelling of the origins of the party had me hypnotized. Like a magician snapping his fingers, his ending left me clueless. What did I have to do with this fantastic tale? They had already dictated the messages, edited the transcripts, even had galleys. What more could they need from me?

It was Diana who answered me. "John, we would like to ask you to introduce us to the world. Would you be so kind as to put into words the story of our coming together? All of us would be so honored if you would."

I dare say it didn't take much for the Party to convince me that I was the best man for the job. What could I say? Coming upon my parents and this distinguished Party of Twelve was indeed a most amazing phenomenon. I am deeply honored to have been asked to be a part of this ambitious work.

Perhaps the most ambitious idea is to simply allow the Party to speak for themselves. Between the twelve of them, they've created a most fascinating book.

Read it carefully, and as my mother would advise me, give it time to sink in. This is perhaps the first time in recorded history that twelve such distinguished people sat down in the Afterlife to record their perceptions of creation as a whole with the intention to influence world peace. But without your help, they will forever remain just words on a page, a weird and mysterious story from beyond the grave.

Diana Spencer & Gianni Versace

July 1, 1961 - August 31, 1997   December 2, 1946 - July 15, 1997

World Peace & A Message For Elton John

Q: Princess Diana, thank you so much for consenting to do this interview. There are so many who are wondering how you are now.

DS: Please, call me Diana.

Q: Diana, tell us about where you are now.

DS: I am in this marvelous place of spirit and acceptance, filled with healing love. There is time to rest here, although, I dare say I've not been getting much rest with all of the work yet to be done.

Q: What kind of work are you doing?

DS: I am working mostly with my children and my family. I have been with the Queen a great deal, and you can see the changes in her lately. She has really become a much more earthy leader in these past few months, don't you think? She seems to be smiling a lot more, then, doesn't she?

Q: And what about your children? What do you do with them?

DS: When one leaves the Earth and passes into spirit, you still retain a connection to those you love, especially as a mother. The love does not stop in death. So there's a natural gravitation to go back to those you love the most to help with their grieving and healing the pain of losing their loved one. My children are very close to me, and my death has, as you can surely imagine, left large holes in their lives. I've been trying to help with the organization of how their new lives will be.

William has always been a very intuitive child. There's so much that the press and the world in general cannot see about what their lives are like. But he sees me in his dreams now and I'm able to help him from there. Harry is taking it all the much harder. He's always been a very compassionate, sensitive young man. But Charles is doing a smashing job of trying to fill an impossible void. He loves those children as much as I do, and he has his own pain to contend with.

My job has been to just be around and try to shine some light into their hearts, to give them the patience to move through time in order to heal.

Q: Is Dodi there with you?

DS: In a sense he is, but he's working in a different arena than I. We see each other and know we are eternally connected. His work now is taking him to a different place than mine.

Q: And what place is that?

DS: He is working more in the peacemaking areas of the Middle East, while I am concentrating primarily on England.

Q: What have you been doing with Queen Elizabeth?

DS: Underneath all the finery and the royal expectations of the Palace, she's always been an ordinary woman. She has never had a chance in her adult life to touch that part of herself. Much of my work with her is helping her to realize that even though she is the leader of this powerful country, she can be that ordinary woman that's inside her. You'll see her now much more relaxed, with more smiles, simpler clothing. If you ask the people around her, especially her personal assistant who has been with her for a long time, you'll find them commenting on this change in her.

She's a very powerful dreamer. She used to talk about her dreams but of course, it could never be leaked that she had dreams that foretold of things that were going to happen. Then she'd be called crazy. She had enough to deal with, between keeping her boys on the up-and-up, and making sure all the proper etiquette and social mores were kept in place.

Contrary to what the press and everyone else thought, the Queen and I had a special relationship. She saw the intrinsic value of what I'd been doing, and she could understand, and even envied a bit, the challenges I had leaving this life of royalty. She even said to me once that she wished on occasion that she, too, could leave that protected public life and if she could do it over, she would live in a little country cottage outside of London and grow a garden of her own. She's a very simple, good-hearted woman who had no idea what being Queen was going to do to her. Now she is trying to get back to that ordinary part of her. I think she's doing quite fabulously, considering.

Q: Di, let's talk about your death. Do you remember what happened to you that night with Dodi?

DS: I have many memories of that night, and I do have to say, I was spared having to remember the horrific parts. Even though I was conscious for awhile, I was already out of my body by the time they found me. For a fleeting second, I returned to my body in the car, like a spot check, to see that yes, I was really dying.

When we left the restaurant, I knew something was going to happen. In fact, for weeks before my death I had had this nagging feeling. I'm not sure how to describe it. It's not like I foresaw my death, but there was this tenderness that pervaded my life. When I was with my children, I felt a kind of urgency. My thoughts were sometimes preoccupied with what would happen to them if I died. I found myself wanting to make peace with Charles in ways that I had never felt before.

I even tried to put some unfinished personal business in order. I asked my assistant to contact some people I had not spoken to in the months before my death.

When we left the restaurant I had a strange feeling, but we had been drinking and laughing at dinner, and everything seemed so "normal." You know, the funny thing about it was, that dinner was a special night for Dodi and me. We had been working through some facets of our relationship that had been very difficult. I love Dodi, and in life I loved him very much, but he was not the love of my life like he felt about me. If you would see his apartment, he had so many pictures of me around. He was such a gallant man, and believed with his whole heart in worshipping the woman he loved, but after the life I had been living, of being held up as an icon, I was looking for a more down-to-earth place. Oddly enough, even in his adoration of me, he gave me that. But we were much more like brother and sister, really, than Romeo and Juliet.

That night at dinner, we had come to this wonderful agreement. I understood that I could not ask him to not worship me, but he agreed that we would try to be more casual in our direction together. I could see it was hard on him, because he wanted me to be this adoring passionate partner, but I simply could not, and that was okay.

When we left the hotel and the photographers started to follow us, we had this discussion in the car about lack of privacy. You must understand, there is a kind of shield one develops when one is in the public eye as much as I had been. Even though there was always an irritation, I had come to a place where I just ignored it. I had to, in order to live my life with any kind of normalcy, which of course was impossible in the position I was in. But when they started to chase us, at first it was a joke to try and outrun them, a sort of, "We'll show them!" There really was a kind of gaiety to it, like, we could do this because we were morally better than they were.

When we got into the tunnel, everything just went black for me. I think that's why Trevor does not remember either. The power of what happened was that it happened so fast. In a matter of a few seconds we hit and spun, and I went black. For me, there was no pain. Even when I was allowed to slip back into my body to be assured that this really was happening, I did not feel pain.

It's very difficult to explain what it's like to die, much less how it feels to die in this accidental way. When things went black, I left my body and was watching the entire incident as if I was hovering over it. It's like I could see through the tunnel, like I had x-ray vision. I saw the photographers coming back and the struggle that ensued. But I was completely detached from it all. It was like watching a movie.

Then I was met by my angel, whom I have known about all my life, and he told me that I had just died. I was amazingly calm, except for the great pull about Harry and William. I wanted to be able to go back for just a moment, because I could not believe I was really dead.

So I was allowed to return to my body. That was when the photographer was taking a picture of me dying through the window of the sedan. I could hear my angel telling me that this was going to be very controversial. I had no feeling one way or the other about his photographing me. I was so much more concerned about my boys.

It's funny, you surely have heard that your life passes before your eyes when you die. What you don't know is, at least with me, I was shown the future also. I suppose it was my angel's way of assuring me that my children were going to be healthy and happy. So I was taken to a place in the future where Harry is older and he is actually carrying on some of the work that I started. William will follow his father more, as part of the lineage of the crown.

That was what I received when I went back into my body. With this reassurance, I left again. It took me some time to come to understand the gravity of the situation. Not that I was in trouble, or that there was a question about my work here. But at first I didn't understand the repercussions of my death all around the world. I was quite astounded with the outpouring of love that people all over the world gave upon my passing.

You see, when you pray, there is a light that is sent up to heaven, and there are great armies and masses of angels waiting to help with prayers. When I passed away, the lights shone for a long time with the prayers of people in every part of the world. I was truly amazed at the range of influence I had had. It touched me so deeply to know that people cared, people I would never have had a chance to meet or talk to. Especially in India.

When people came to the Palace and left all those flowers, I was overwhelmed. It made me feel much more connected to my life, to all the times I doubted what I was doing. I could see then that all the horse feathers I had to put up with as princess were all worth it.

So I want to tell the world, never doubt the range of influence you have on the people around you. Don't underestimate how far a kind gesture will go.

Q: Princess Di, do you think you were murdered?

DS: What you have to understand is, there were so many threats against us. I mean, Dodi had an entire collection of threat letters and his office often got phone calls, and I was always getting those kinds of threats against me. It's not hard to concoct a scheme that someone was behind this, what with the many people you could point fingers at.

The hardest part is the accusations against Dodi's father. He might have been a very hard businessman and unorthodox, but he was really a delightful man who loved his son very deeply. He also always made me feel as if I was very special to him, not because I was princess but because I was someone who loved his son.

To answer the question, no it was not murder.

Q: Then why do you think this happened? Why do you think you were taken at such a vital age, what with your kids and new life just beginning.

DS: *[laughing]* You want me to explain to you how God's mind works? I'm not sure anyone is qualified to discuss that!

But I can say this: there is an incredible amount of order in the Afterlife. It's simply fascinating to watch how one event on one side of the world indirectly influences events on the other side of the world. I truly wish I could explain how all this works, but, well, I believe you will all someday see it for yourself. *[smiling]*

I do know that this was a perfect time for my passing. Even though I had no idea the influence I had on the world, it was made perfectly clear when I died. As I said, I was overwhelmed by the outpouring of love.

I do not believe I had to be taken in order to be some kind of martyr. That is just the by-product of the divine timing. The truth is, this was part of my destiny. In some deep soul place, I knew that I would be taken at this age. So I did all that I could before leaving to make the most of my position and my power. I was almost driven in those last years of my life to touch as many people as I could. And I do mean touch. If you see news clips or photos of my travels around the world, you'll see me touching people. I was not someone who liked to hug or get especially close to the public, but I did like to touch them, simply. I did love to hold the babies. They are the light of the world. I still believe that the children need the most championing.

But in the last year of my life, I fought for my power so that I could use it to its fullest extent. At first, I didn't really understand why I was fighting for my position. Inside I really wanted to chuck it all and get a little cottage on the Seine and remove myself completely from the public eye. So for awhile, through the divorce and dissolution of my princess-hood, I was conflicted as to why I was being driven to make the demands of the Palace that I did.

But as soon as the fight was over and the concessions were made, it became clear to me that I could not run away from public life, as much as I wanted to with all my heart. I truly believe that some part of me knew I had to make the most of my position. Again, I did not know consciously that I was going to die, but some part of me influenced my conscious thinking to make the most of my power.

Q: Is Gianni there with you?

DS: Why, yes, he is! And we have been having quite the time of things here, although his passing was a little more turbulent than mine. But I will let him speak to you.

Q: Gianni, how do you feel about what happened to you? And how do you feel about your killer.

GV: This is again a difficult thing to explain. Sometimes when we are human, we have these ideas about what it is like to die. But I am finding that, once in the realm of spirit, things are so different than we ever imagine them to be while we are living in the flesh.

The murder itself was gruesome and horrifying. I have not been so scared. It happened very quickly, from the time it started. Like Diana, I was not made to endure a great deal of pain, although if I could conjure the human physical memories of the experience, I am quite sure it would be extremely pained.

But this I do know and that is, the young man who committed the murder, who is also in this realm of spirit, is undergoing an experience here that is quite fitting for what happened. I'm not saying he is being tormented or has gone to hell, but his own actions, when he was living his life, have come back to haunt him.

This is what hell is. Believe me, there is not some place that is set aside like we were raised to believe and saw in paintings, that place that is somehow conceived as underground and filled with fire. Hell is something that surrounds the souls of those like that young man. He created this energy for himself, and now he has to pass through it, directed at himself.

I have absolutely nothing but compassion for this young man. He was actually very much like me in many ways. He did not have the wherewithal or the connections to power that allowed me to make the rise into the world as I did. But he had the same tormented childhood as I did. He was not accepted by his parents for who he was, and therefore did not learn to accept himself. But at every turn, his life became a torture chamber. He fell in love several times and was thwarted by the objects of his affections.

But underneath his pain, he was a loving and compassionate young man. He had killed others before he got to me, and by that time, he was already creating his own hell for himself.

If there is one thing I want to tell the world, it's not to judge him. Forgive him and send prayers of compassion to those who are his family, for they are in their own kind of hell, too.

DS: Yes, we both agree that it is very important at this juncture to forgive those people who you think did this to us. Especially when it comes to the press, who are getting a lot of the blame for what happened to me. No, I wish I did not have to contend with the kind of privacy invasion that occurred to me in my life, and I certainly want my children to be spared from that, but in the bigger picture, from God's mind, this is not about blaming them for my death.

There is going to be a very profound change in how the world looks at privacy of world figures. We are working, both Gianni and I, from this place, to help this change come into effect. And the change begins with the average person understanding that every star, every princess, every entertainer who seems bigger than life and puts themselves out into the spotlight is also just an ordinary person. There will come a time when people will understand that, and it won't take away from the beauty or mystique that person offers. And it will help to stop the perpetuation of the invasions of privacy that happen.

Q: Gianni, will you speak to us about the fashion industry? The focus on ultra-thin models is not only putting emphasis on outward appearance and not inward character, but creating impossible ideals for women in relationship to their bodies.

GV: As a promoter of this "uber-thin" model, first let me tell you the dynamic from the side of compassion.

The fashion world is one place where homosexuality is accepted within the infrastructure. Here we have created for ourselves a place of safety, us being this group of misfits, outcasts, what some would call "deviants." Others who do not fit in find their way into this fashion world. This is a place where the "beautiful deviants" at least can be taken care of by their own, by others who understand the power of being physically beautiful but socially unacceptable. When a model cannot stand, for being too weak from not eating, or drugs, the community understands, and provides a place to lie down. No, it is not the "politically correct" way to create this kind of enclave, but that is what we have done. But trust me, everyone pays the price by becoming enslaved by this mechanism of cultural programming that is projecting that very sickness back onto culture.

How can the very people who grace the covers of national magazines be, on one hand, the idols of bodily icons to aspire to and, on the other hand, the deviant homosexual drug addicts making ungodly amounts of money? Do you understand how very surreal the fashion world is? On some subterranean level, the fashion industry is tormenting culture, especially women, by creating desperately thin models and displaying them on the cover of magazines in the supermarket lines, as if this size 2 depiction of women is common and every day. When was the last time you talked in person to someone who wore size 2? Unless you are a part of the industry, they are rare in the ordinary world. Fashion has a chokehold on the subconscious of women.

My personal push into the industry started from my own inner sense of waywardness. Rising to the top of this world that protected, even encouraged people to overlook their personal health to fit into a tiny, miniature form was very destructive. And yet, in many ways, it was one way for me, who felt so unacceptable, to not only find a place to fit, but then turn around and rule the very "innards" of the society that was rejecting me.

Yes, there is a deep, subconscious cry that comes from the darkness of many people in the world of fashion. What this cry says is, "If I cannot fit into culture, I will create my own 'haute-couture,' I will write my own rules." We send outrageous fashion down the runways, knowing all of the world will watch and try to become those things.

Within the walls of this enclave there is a need for some light. I am hoping this book will help to shine, yes, even into fashion, some of this peace for the world.

Q: Gianni, you and Di and Elton John were all very close. Can you tell us about your relationship to him? Are you working with him, too, at this time?

GV: Oh my, yes! We are all still as close as ever.

DS: The three of us, when we got together, we were like little children. There was a kind of unspoken knowledge we had amongst us about what it was like to be so well known. So when we got together we could all let our hair down.

GV: We laughed so much together. Elton really is such a delightfully humorous person. I love him so much. We both understood what being so in the spotlight and holding a sexual orientation that went against the norm did to our perception of our worth. I found a great comfort in my friendship with him because of that, and he in me, too.

DS: We often talked about the spiritual nature of things. We loved to believe we could talk to those who had died. Elton even called a psychic in once.

We were interested in the workings of the universe, more like Albert Einstein. The only problem was that this psychic was very much oriented to seeing the details of life. But in the details, she saw, well, as you can imagine, some fairly dastardly things. So she did not want to say anything, and the situation became uncomfortable.

GV: I have always looked to astrology for guidance in my life. I knew that my life was going to end before it did. I even told my assistant that I thought there was something in the offing for me. But you know, your close people never want to believe those things. They cannot fathom their lives without the ones they love, so there was not much room for me to talk about it.

But the three of us talked about what if one of us died. We made each other promise that we would somehow come back and give a message. The truth is, both Diana and myself have been with Elton, too. He has been devastated, and the trouble we are having is that he is so shaken by our deaths that every time we appear to him, he relives his deep grief.

DS: Yes, it's difficult at this juncture to truly get a message through to him. Not that he doesn't believe in this Afterlife, but for him, now, it doesn't matter because in his life he is without his closest friends. I have been working in his dreams and being close to him that way. Sometimes he even sees me in his house. I believe he knows it's me, but at this point in his grieving process there is not much we can do but wait.

GV: This is why we have connected with Barbara. We believe she is able to get this message out to the world. She is someone that was referred to us. <<laughing>> Yes, it's true, our angels referred us to her!

Q: Is there anything you would like to say to Elton? Is there some message we can deliver to him that will help him in his grieving process?

DS: Well, first of all, Fluffy, we want to tell you that we really are here! Don't doubt for a minute, chum, that we aren't around you and helping you with your writing.

I want to say, Elton, you knew I was there in the song. I always loved that song the best of all of your songs, and I know why you played that as a tribute to me. You often said I was the light of the world. I would laugh and say you were just teasing, but you insisted that someday I would know how much influence I have. Well, I want to tell you Elton, I know that now. I know that I have been a light to many, many people in the world. And you singing "Candle In The Wind" only spread that light even further, to every corner of the world, even the places I missed.

And you, too, are a light to the world, my friend, and please don't ever forget how smashingly beautiful you are. You, too, have already touched so many people.

GV: Elton, you will come back from this and go on to produce your most magnificent works. Remember how you used to tell me my best was yet to come? I know that now, too...and I have committed to working closely with you. Both Diana and I are staying close to you and are going to use the great influence we now have to assist you with this project you are planning.

And we would like you to know that, if you thought we were influential when we were alive, you must know that now we have some very close and even more powerful friends willing to help in many, *many* ways.

Q: Is there any last message you two would like to give the world?

GV: Never underestimate your own power. Life is too short, even if you live to be very old. You just never know when you will be snatched from life, and taken away. So give your life everything you can, and do not be afraid to dream big.

DS: I would only like to say that the individual is where world peace starts. You can make a very big difference in your world. Touch as many people as you can, make peace on as many fronts as you have. And understand that, even after life, in death, you go on working and loving.

There is great peace here. I would never have known this while in life. So if you are reading this, know that your life is precious, too. You don't have to be a princess or famous designer or singer to make a difference. In fact, peace really rests in the hands of the commoners. We are all commoners in heaven. And we are all stars. Love yourselves and each other and you *will* make a difference.

Nicole Brown Simpson

May 19, 1959 ~ June 12, 1994

Race Relations & Domestic Abuse

Q: We'd like to thank you for being here with us and we look forward to getting your message out to people. Of course, we all want to know what happened that evening, but more importantly, what's happening with your kids? Are you able to help them from where you are?

NBS: It really is quite an honor to be able to have a voice this way. You must know this just isn't an everyday occurrence for most of us.

There's so much to say. Even here in spirit now, I'm still undergoing a healing process. My work in healing myself is also affecting my children. Right now, most of my focus is going directly towards them.

I ache for them, to be able to hold them again and touch them. They're very vacant right now. To look at them, if you didn't know them, you'd think there's something terribly wrong but you wouldn't be able to say what it is. The scary part is, they haven't gone through any great grieving period. This is the work I have to do with them, to help them grieve.

When all the commotion began, even though they were sheltered from the press and the explosion in the media, that sheltering kept them out of touch with their feelings. It's hard to explain. You don't want the children exposed to all the gore and the details and the kind of exposé that went on. But because their father was taken away from them right after their mother died such a horrible death, well, they went into deep denial. It was very surreal for them.

Understand, though, that their entire lives were about being in denial. They knew what O.J. did to me. They were well aware of his abuse, his threats. He hurt them, too. But in order to cope, they had to deny. Even in all the violence at home, they loved him. But having that basis of denial doesn't help them when it comes to their own grieving.

Now I talk to them in the privacy of their own lives. I told them not to talk about this communication we have. I understand the kind of farce that it might evoke in the tabloids. If you're a mother, you understand, you want to protect your children from pain. You want to save them from having to go through difficult things. My job has been to get them to go into their pain. I know it will help them heal from this tremendous burden that's been thrown upon them, but it's a difficult job.

Now they're faced with this big custody battle. Can you imagine my dilemma? I certainly don't want to deprive them of their father and yet, how can I entrust them into his hands? He murdered me. I don't trust him with them. And yet, I have to help them heal from not only the wounds of my murder, but the harm that he has inflicted on them with his lies and his greed. This truly is what living in hell must be like.

My only hope is that as I continue to work and be with them, giving them all my focus, that we're working hand in hand to heal each other on deeper levels.

Q: Talking about the press, why do you think it was so important for the press to make you and your sister out to be the bad guys? Do you think it was for the sensationalism, for the story, or do you feel it was easier to make it seem like you almost deserved what happened?

NBS: Isn't that what the press does? Looks for every angle? If you're on one side of the road, they'll stand on the other side of the road and try to paint a picture of exactly what you aren't. You remember what happened in the press when Mother Teresa died. Even she was given the old heave ho, a woman of such great stature.

Me, I was basically just an ordinary woman. I had beauty and I married a very prominent and well-respected man. We had an interracial marriage; right there are several angles that the press could use, whether it be that I was the vamp and he was the football hero, or he was the nigger and I was the virgin. The press was going to spin whatever they needed at the time to make themselves be important, because that's what their job has turned into.

The press in this country has become a strange and powerful force. My sister, who fought tirelessly to get the truth out to the press to exonerate who I was, got slapped in the face again and again, despite her grief. She wasn't trying to make me out to be something that I wasn't. She was merely trying to show the world what I truly had been and what I truly had been going through. That's part of why I've chosen to step forward in this way. The system that's in place here, not just the press, but a lot of the cultural media in the world today is structured in such a way that ordinary people can't be heard. People like O.J. become beyond the reach of the ordinary, as you see by the outcome of what happened.

The press is undergoing a huge change right now. People just aren't standing for the kind of sickness they've been generating in the culture. The system as a whole is meant to generate confusion, instant gratification and to take hold of the minds of ordinary people. Imagine if the press had morals! Imagine if it was dedicated to being part of the solution to all of culture's ills and not perpetuating them. The press right now is far too powerful for its own good.

Q: Was race a major factor in what happened? Also, race doubly affects the children. On top of the grief of losing their parents, what are their issues having to do with the fact that they're biracial?

NBS: First of all, my children will never be able to be ordinary people. Not just because of their interracial parentage, but because of all that's happened to them. Their family life was chaotic from the time they were brought into the world. It wasn't like they ever had a normal life, considering the side-by-side violence and prestige that went on in our home and the lack of privacy that we had to contend with. Yet, because they were raised in that environment, they became accustomed to it. Their father was in the limelight. Every time we went out, they were constantly being rushed from one place to the next to avoid photographers and attention and all the things that followed us around. This became a very normal part of their lives.

That aspect of what happened to my children laid the groundwork for a kind of denial that goes on with them, a denial that they are ordinary children. It's confusing for them on a deeper level to know who they are.

There was also the part of O.J. and my relationship that was racially complex. I don't believe that people understand the depth of this complexity that went on with us as an interracial couple.

The psychology that O.J. was dealing with was very subversive. On his level of thinking, he was someone who came from what was basically a prejudiced situation against white people. He himself was not necessarily someone who exhibited those qualities of being racist. In fact, many of his good friends were white. It wasn't the kind of racism that made him crusade against whites as a race that was keeping his people down. There was a reverse psychology in play with him.

In his early childhood, there was often talk around his supper table about the suppression that the white people were promoting onto the black culture. His mother's side of the family was not very complimentary, to say the least, about the condition of culture and how the white race has dominated. That's not to say she didn't have compassion in her heart and she wasn't a loving person, or didn't care about her children. And it's also not to say that she didn't have a point.

The point I'm making is that it was a very covert kind of racism. His feelings early on in his life, not so much what he thought consciously, but his feelings were that he had to gain the favor of the ruling group. It wasn't that he felt he needed white people in his life to get ahead. He was always a very ambitious man, and could set his sights on whatever he wanted. From an early age he worked hard to get where he did. But when he got into the echelons of power that were going to help propel him to the places he wanted to go, he made friends with the white ruling class for a specific purpose: to be able to conquer it. He did that quite successfully, as you can see by his track record in his life. He overcame a lot of what held him back because he was a black man.

What happened in the privacy of our home was that I became the object of the subliminal anger that he had towards that white culture that simultaneously kept him down, and also propped him up. This was very confusing for him in a deep place inside. It wasn't that he wasn't mean to other women in his life that happened to be black, but because of the intense nature of our relationship, because we had two children together and were closer than any of the other black women who had been in his life, it began to find a place to manifest.

The domestic abuse that I experienced and his anger, when he lost his mind, often became racial and sexist. It was such a complicated mix of psychology, pain and desire within him that I didn't know how to explain that to anyone. I certainly wasn't going to come out with the idea that he needed to use me as a whipping post for the idea of race relations, but sometimes that was what it was.

Q: Do you feel like you were a trophy wife?

NBS: When we first met, we did have that passionate period of having a love affair. But it was so unreal to me. The worlds that he moved in didn't really support honest emotions. At that time, I didn't really feel like a trophy wife.

I did feel that, in the latter part of our relationship, after the kids were born, he was burdened by the idea of fatherhood. He supported the idea of it, but when it came to actually having a full, solid hand in raising the kids, he left a lot of that to me. I felt more like a neglected part of his life.

Yes, we would go out, and I was a beautiful woman,

and he did look a lot better with me on his arm. Whenever there was violence at home, and then we had to go out in public, the least of my concerns was that I was a trophy wife. I was the wife of an abuser, but, no one believed me, not his male friends, not the media, not anyone on his side of the fence. My family knew, and they tried with all their might to get me out of that situation. But, as with most abused women, there is a kind of hopeless addiction to the cycle of violence. Being merely a trophy wife would have been a walk in the park compared to being the brunt of his anger, the punching bag for his frustrations, then the Madonna of his redemption.

Q: Now that you're where you are, and you can look back and see the purpose of your life, do you feel like you lived to learn a specific life lesson?

NBS: I don't think anyone ever comes into life thinking that they're going to be murdered by their husband. Certainly there was a powerful theme that ran through my life. I was nurtured to be dependent upon a relationship and a man. I was taught, because I was a beautiful woman, how to use that beauty.

Looking back, I understand the purpose of what I had to go through in my life to get here. It's difficult to explain until you've passed on. It's hard to explain how you look back and see your life. It's not what you'd think. It's much more complete. You don't have the questions that you had in life, when you're going through a painful time and wondering, "Why is this happening to me, why me?" You don't have those questions here.

In that sense, I have come to an understanding. There was a very important purpose for what happened with O.J. and me, and the murder and the attention. Think about how much influence that crime had on almost everyone in America and around the world. People watched, people talked, they got mad, they were happy, they rallied. It was a very galvanizing affair. Did I wish to be murdered and taken from my children? No, but from this place, do I see the purpose and the importance and the influence that I had on history? Yes, I very clearly understand about that.

Q: Can you see any beauty that's going to come of this?

NBS: Beauty? In being brutally murdered by my husband? In being taken from my babies while they are still so young? It's difficult for me, in light of the fact that my children are now faced with so many challenges, to see any beauty in this.

But when I can back up three steps and become the fuller spirit that I am, and touch upon the God-part of me, I do see that the influence of this murder has reached around the world. This tragedy brought a lot of emotion to different people, not just women who may be in abusive relationships. If it scares them to a point where they want to do something before it's too late, that's a beautiful thing. If even one woman reads my story, and makes the choice to get out of the relationship before she, too, gets killed, than I feel at least what happened to me can help someone else. There is a kind of beauty in that.

For the most part, there's beauty in the difficult things in life. The work I'm doing with my children is difficult, I admit, even from this place. But at least from this point of view, I can appreciate where I am now. You think you go to a place after you die where there's just peace and no turbulence, but I'm finding that I have a long way to go with that. I'm going to stick close to my children while I go through that.

The awareness of race relations, not necessarily as seen through my relationship with him, but as seen through his relationship to the world and culture, has certainly changed the lives of many people. You can't discount that because of the tragic nature of what happened.

Q: Ron Goldman was obviously there inadvertently, and I'm sure that he was never meant to be murdered, but in the end he was. Do you see him now? What's going on with him now?

NBS: He was certainly in the wrong place at the wrong time, and yet from an energetic perspective, this plays into a part of his life and his spiritual being that's very important to him. He's very close with his family. There's a lot of healing that's gone on in his family because of the fight that he's been doing with them to clear his name through having some kind of responsibility put on O.J. You have to understand the amount of energy that the Goldman family put into the fight to clear our names and get O.J. to take responsibility for what he did. Just because all the trials are over doesn't mean the healing is done. Ron is working very closely with them.

Q: Now, about O.J. I imagine that his life is not a pleasant one right now. Do you see him? Can you see what's going on with him emotionally?

NBS: The odd thing is, I am very close to him. A day doesn't go by where we don't communicate. He's living in hell, but on a deep level he truly has convinced himself that he didn't do this. He's had to do this for such a long time that he actually believes it now. He remembers a difference occurrence. Even when he remembers the murder, he remembers it in a different way than it actually happened, in order to maintain his sanity. Having to be in such deep denial is preventing him from feeling the spontaneous, real feelings of his life. He's basically dead inside. He often thinks of killing himself.

I've been trying to help with forgiveness. His torture is really going to come after he dies. Then there's no hiding from the truth of his own emotions and the repercussions of his own actions.

In the meantime, it's very important for my healing and for the healing of my children that I do everything I can to help him forgive himself so that it will have a reciprocal effect on the children. But frankly, I'm still working on forgiving him. It's complicated. But just so you should know, there's a large number of angels working with all of us around this.

Q: We talked about your work with your sister. We don't really hear much from her right now. She seemed to be in such a fragile state, how she's doing?

NBS: She's actually come quite a long way. The second trial was a great victory for her. Her work after the murder and all of the emotional energy that went into her crusade to help the world really understand what really happened was quite healing. She didn't see it that way, because she was in such pain the whole time. Once the second trial was finished and the truth was at least recognized, there was a great closure for her. She's now left with a pain in her life that really didn't have anything to do with me.

That was the difficult part about her crusade. She was pushed from a place of pain of losing her sister. We were fairly close. The exoneration left her with other things in her life that were painful. But what she'd been through, the trial and the book, the tour and all the public speaking that she did strengthened her.

She has a couple of projects in the fire and you'll be hearing again from her soon.

Q: That evening of the crime, how is it that he was able to attack you and nobody could hear you scream, that nobody witnessed it, even though there were people on the block and you had neighbors? How was he able to do this without being caught?

NBS: Remember, this was not a spontaneous crime. He thought about killing me for a long time. Looking back, I can see many instances where he'd hinted that something was going to happen, aside from when he would scream that he was going to kill me. There were times when he would be very secretive about where he had been, or he would just show up and try to convince me to come back to him. It felt like he was trying to lure me back into his trust so he could then pounce.

The fact that Ron was there that night complicated his well-laid plans, but because he was so intent on killing, I see now he had no problem spontaneously taking Ron out, too. At first, O.J. approached me from the shadows, very civilly. But he didn't see Ron at first. He didn't come racing out of the bushes waving the knife, but I could tell that he was angry, pent up. Although he was very controlled, I'd felt this many times before. It was a part of the cycle of his abuse. I knew something was deeply troubling him, like he had been obsessing on something.

When he came up to me, I knew something was wrong, and immediately told him to go away. I said I didn't want to see him. His first words were about how he wanted to reconcile. When he saw me with Ron, all of that rage in him just decompressed. He was a strong man to begin with, big and powerful and burly. He was close enough to me so that by the time he actually had contact with me and his hand was over my mouth, he was unleashed.

Ron tried to step in. The wounds inflicted on Ron were enough to debilitate him, to take him out for the moment. Then, after O.J. was through with me, he did Ron in and got away.

Part of why no one heard us was the seclusion of the neighborhood that we lived in. It was the kind of neighborhood designed to be private, so that we didn't have to know what our neighbors were doing. That was part of the surprise. Part of it was that he planned it for a long time. When he realized Ron was there, that made him all the more angry. Not just the jealousy, because he assumed that Ron and I were having a relationship that we weren't. It goes back to race relations. Here I was, someone who was supposed to help him fit into white culture, and yet underneath it I was one of them, another white whore. In the privacy of our own home, I became the enemy. And now I'd betrayed him by being with someone of a different race than he was. You can begin to see how complicated the whole thing was. In his rage, he was able to kill us very quickly.

He would have killed me anyway, even if Ron wasn't there.

Q: What was he wearing?

NBS: He was wearing a wet suit that he'd stolen from the set of a movie, "Frogman." It was the movie he was working on about six months before the murder. Ask the people from the movie. They had a suit made just for him, and it just disappeared. The film people had to have a new one made, and it was very expensive.

I'm telling you, he'd been entertaining ideas of how to murder me for years before it happened. Even when times were happy, whenever we'd fight, he'd throw it in my face, this thing about killing me. Once, he locked me in a closet while he sat watching football. As I was screaming to get out, he systematically told me exactly how it was going to be. He said it would be late at night, and that he would make it look like someone else did it, that he would get everyone he knew to vouch for him. He even told me he had taken this diving suit, and that when I least expected it, he would get me. Sometimes he would tell me he was going to blow my brains out, he was big into guns. Other times he would say it was going to be stabbing, just quietly slitting my throat. He was sick, a very, very sick man.

Q: Were you in the courtroom during the trial?

NBS: That's an interesting question. After I passed out of my body so quickly and unexpectedly, it was a great shock to me that I actually had died. I hovered for awhile around my body and around Ron. His spirit was separated from me at that time. It wasn't as if we died together and turned back to see what had happened to us. I was very much alone except for the angels.

You always hear about that, being greeted in death

by angels and loved ones. It's true. The angels are a powerful force and comfort in death. You don't have to die a peaceful death in order to be greeted this way.

Because I died quickly and unexpectedly, it took some time to really understand where I was and what I could do now. My heart was with my children. I really wasn't concerned about whether O.J. was going to get what he deserved. I was focusing on my children.

From this place, I was able to be with them through the trial and do my best to give them the kind of comfort they needed now that they had no parents.

I was privy to what was going on with the trial, but I really didn't care. I was with my children. But yes, there was a part of me that wanted the world to know what he had done, not just in killing me, but all the things that happened that led up to my murder. That's why my sister was so motivated. I was working with her to get that information out to the public.

Q: Do you feel like the case was bungled? Or do you feel like this was part of the master plan, like this is going to make society look more carefully at justice? Or do you feel there were just mistakes made?

NBS: Yes, absolutely, the case was a farce. The lawyers for the prosecution were so wrapped up in themselves and their own careers they really didn't put into it what lawyers in an ordinary murder case would. If it had been conducted like any other murder case, where the focus wasn't on the lawyers but on the case, it might have come to a different conclusion.

The judge was also not truly interested in the fair trial. Of course, look what he had to work with. He must have felt like a daycare worker some days, the way everyone was acting, like this was all about them, and not about bringing this murder to justice. I think America should study these trials as a foremost example of misuse of the criminal justice system.

In a perfect world, all the bungling mistakes wouldn't have been made. Justice would have been served by convicting him of the crime he committed and put him into jail, maybe even giving him the death sentence. Then O.J. could have been put out of his own misery, and the message sent to abusers everywhere would have been different: Beware! You cannot abuse women and get away with it. Oh well...

However, from the Afterlife, I can see there is a master plan in effect, and perhaps his getting off and having to live with himself will be hell enough. Every time he looks into the faces of his children, he will see me staring back, like a mirror. He will never forget.

Ultimately, though, I think the way the case played out was purposeful. Many people were touched by it. There was a lot of controversy and consequently, a lot of awareness raised by the way it ended. Now, in retrospect, from this place, for me the lessons are forgiveness and coming to understand what I'm supposed to do now.

Q: We'd like to thank you for speaking with us and close with our appreciation. Do you have any last words that you'd like to say?

NBS: I would just like to say that I think it's very important for parents to understand that they are teaching through example to their children. Whether you're an interracial couple, a divorced couple sharing custody of the children, a single parent, two people in love, or fighting, it doesn't matter. Every action that you do teaches your children that action. They learn best through example.

So maybe the best thing you can do is to concentrate on what your own actions are. Get to know yourself, examine your own actions and exert a little more power over what you choose to do with your life, how you choose to act out your emotions and feelings, and what you are willing to give back to the world.

Remember, your children will carry on your inner life as well. That's the importance of making sure your inner life is as strong and clear as it can be.

JOHN F. KENNEDY & JACQUELINE ONASSIS

May 29, 1917 ~ November 22, 1963   July 28, 1929 ~ May 19, 1994

Politics, Press & Publishing

Q: Hello, Mr. President. It's an honor to have you here with us. I'm going to go straight into this. Let's start out with, who killed you?

JFK: This was a function of an organization of people who were not necessarily in the public eye. All of the theories involving the government and Lyndon were only partially correct. There was a group of individuals who were a very high-powered circle of political sympaticos involved at various levels with senators and congressmen and also myself.

While they had influences in the inner circles of the political arenas, they weren't directly involved in those arenas. They were more like lobbyists or "friends of" and had a very heavy agenda when it came to various political and economic issues.

Contrary to what some of the theories have been, there wasn't one galvanizing event that inspired them to want to remove me from office. There were several disagreements and experiences between the office of the presidency. Their circle then built a plan to do what they did. One of these things that inspired them was a little known project I was working on to reduce their power and influence.

Remember, back then, there was an entirely different political atmosphere. The public was naive about how the government was run. The common, ordinary citizen was not privy to what you're all aware of now. The lobbyists were much less prominent in public knowledge then, and they didn't have the kind of scrutiny from outside observers as they do now. Now they're out front, less subterranean, but they still influence the politicians. Prior to my assassination, we were having discussions in the Oval Office about how to deal with this outside influence on the political system.

I was caught between a rock and a hard place. While I was working to reveal this hidden influence, I had also grown up with the acceptance of that relationship between government and business. My father's relationships with big business gave me a glimpse into the corruption. There was always money being passed under the table and favors being done for powerful men in the business world.

This powerful circle of business men who were based in Texas were not very happy with my ideological plans to uncover their presence. They had, after all, helped to elect me.

I was not the only one, others were working on this, too, journalists, the press. Back then, the press was much more ethical in many ways. They had at the heart of their intentions an interest in uncovering the truth of what was happening in the country, not just sensationalizing things to create interest, to bolster ratings. Their job was about getting information in the best way they could to the American people.

If you look back on the records at the time, you'll find several journalists who had been uncovering these things also met with an untimely demise.

Keep in mind, you must look past the fictionalization of what happened to me, and all the theories of why I was assassinated. Look at a combination of influences, rather than just one conspiracy theory involving the government. They were in on this, but they weren't organizing it. They were agreeing to turn their heads to what was happening rather than being the source of the conspiracy.

Q: Was there more than one gunman?

JFK: Yes, there were actually five gunmen planted in the area to await my arrival. They had a series of different commands or signals to each other. If one plan wasn't going to work out because one of the gunman was situated in too many people, then they had a number of backup plans that could go into effect. But the signals got crossed, so that rather than just one of them shooting, one of them shot and in the excitement, three different people actually did the shooting.

Q: Were all of the gunmen then killed in some fashion?

JFK: Yes.

Q: I saw a documentary once that showed how all of the people connected died a mysterious death. There must have been at least 25 people who had died in mysterious car accidents and what not. Were they all part of the conspiracy?

JFK: No, not that many, there just weren't that many people who had to be removed at the end. The inner core of this circle was very tight, much like an American businessmen's mafia. They were very thorough and efficient in getting this done and did it in a way that involved the least number of people possible. Some of the people who were involved in the later things like losing documents or creating diversion didn't have to be removed in the end because of the low-level of association they had with the circle.

Q: Approximately how many people died in addition to yourself?

JFK: There were probably about ten people.

Q: What was the ultimate goal? You explained about the lobbyists and all, but what was the ultimate goal whereby they killed ten people? Was it simply to get someone else in power that was under their thumb?

JFK: Yes, this was the ultimate goal. Here I was, from the Northeast, an Irish Catholic, bringing with me a glamour and a new perspective to the position of President of the United States. Even though I myself was involved in various levels of deception, I also brought new life to American politics and a new light to the American people. My goal to touch ordinary American people was very pure. I had that truth within me. This was one reason why I was so popular. I could touch the man on the street even though my entire life was lived within the confines of a very wealthy and powerful family. I had a sincerity about this mission that allowed me to really make a difference.

My presidency was indeed a turning point for American politics. We were ushering in a new openness and communication. Before that, yes, people loved their presidents, but I was elected during a change in the American culture to open up the government to the ordinary people. This didn't fit well with the inner circle who wanted to subversively control without being challenged. Surely having the government open to more public scrutiny would reveal the illegalities that this group and others were involved in.

There was also a long-standing push that started before I came into office to escalate and continue the war in Vietnam. Those in the inner circle were very much invested in keeping the war going. Some were arms dealers. Others had lucrative business in that part of the world, including the sale of opium and heroin, among other legitimate corporations.

When the French were still in the war in the '50s, they were sympathetic to Western businessmen's financial prosperity because of the cheap labor, lax exportation laws, low cost of goods, and corruption. It was a lucrative climate in the international market. Remember, though, the world then was not as small as it is today. Communications were not anywhere near as sophisticated. The people in the inner circle were very heavily invested in that area, and could keep those dealings out of the news. Couple this with all the "gentlemen's agreements" with the press, and here were the perfect elements to assure their control.

With my elimination, they planned to, first of all, retain the positions of power they had manifested over many years. They also wanted to keep this war going to protect their interests and generate an atmosphere in the country conducive to all levels of their businesses, not just those involved in the military. Farming was a transitional enterprise at this time as well. Inner circle corporations began buying up many of the family farms. This was the beginning of delocalizing government and communities.

Q: How do you feel about the direction that the Kennedy family has taken in the last 15 years or so?

JFK: Since my death, I've continued a close association with my entire family, but mostly with Jackie and my children. They've all been challenged by so many changes. When Bobby died, the family structure started to unravel. It was just too shocking on the heels of what had happened to me.

My children were not the hardest hit. They have a grounding that's almost supernatural, considering what they've been through. That was, of course, due to Jackie, and her dedication to raising those two to be as "normal" as possible.

Even through all the tragedy, the children of my brothers and sisters are actually dealing with it all as best they can. There's a stability amongst them that comes from this overpowering sense of family. Not that everyone's perfect, or that there aren't any casualties from being a Kennedy, certainly. But when someone in the family is stricken with an ill-fated circumstance— alcoholism, untimely death, mental illness, nervous breakdown—what isn't always seen is the powerful, deeply-rooted sense of true family that runs through the many generations. There's a powerful strength and resilience in that force that the family draws on.

My presence in the family, even after my death, has added stability. I'm actively working to keep those family ties armed with love, faith, hope, and an understanding that we are bigger than the challenges that face us. We are never given more than we can handle. We are given this much so that, from our human condition, we don't just meet the challenge but overtake the challenge.

I believe that our family has done just that.

Q: You talked about how the press is different now than it was then. You're obviously aware of the Clinton sex scandal. How do you feel about that?

JFK: This is a good example of how the press has changed over the course of time to become an instrument of their own devices. Today, the importance of the president's private life has been used as a tool to play the country against itself. That is the greatest tragedy of this situation.

President Clinton is, like me, someone in a pivotal place in time. He has chosen to put himself in a place that might appear to be compromising of his ideals and directives. Cultural dictates of 1998 say that he's hurting himself and the presidency, ruining himself with his indiscretions.

In reality, he has chosen to come to this chair with all that he is and all that he has. Again, an ordinary human being, someone who does not profess to be perfect, he doesn't insist that he has no foibles. This doesn't mean that he wants to allow his private inner life to be sacrificed at the altar of public scrutiny. Yet he knows he's in this position to change that, too.

When I was president, there were many more "gentleman's agreements" between the press and those in office. This may or may not have been a good thing. I only know that my indiscretions couldn't have taken place in today's White House because there are no gentleman's agreements anymore.

Q: For example, it would be very difficult for Bill Clinton to have an affair with Madonna?

JFK: It would be impossible for that to take place as quietly as my relationship with Norma Jean took place.

Q: When a president makes a commitment to office and also makes a commitment of fidelity to his wife, the American people should expect him to honor the commitment to the office but not the commitment to the wife?

JFK: An American president makes a commitment to the people to serve out the job of President to the very best of his ability. He makes a commitment to his wife to serve her to the best of his ability as a husband and a partner. These are two reciprocal areas, but they don't become hinged on one another.

Looking at it your way, you should then be able to say that if the president committed a major error in foreign policy that his wife should then be able to divorce him?

Q: I get your point. Will what President Clinton is experiencing be helpful to open people's eyes to these issues?

JFK: What President Clinton is going through is affecting so many more levels of society than you can imagine. He is bringing a deeper reflection to America, and I'm not talking about his personal decisions to have an affair and try to keep it secret. I'm talking about what the media has been doing to his private life.

The gentlemen's agreements in effect when I was in office weren't just to hide unsavory details of a private life. The press used to turn away because those topics didn't fall under the category of political news back then. That kind of information was for the scandal sheets. You weren't a "real" journalist if all you talked about was a man's private life. Back then, the press was about the scandal of politics, not the scandal of the politicians. Everyone wanted to see Kruschev, no one really wanted to know about his sex life. Today's culture has integrated sex far more openly, therefore, it seems like a piece of news to know with whom a famous politician slept. It has become news as entertainment as opposed to news as education.

Q: Do you think that one of the goals of our society should be to overhaul the media?

JFK: Within the complicated set of circumstances that make up society, an overhauling is needed of the moral value system placed upon individuals within the whole of culture. Part of this means giving up the security of an outside authority to dictate to you what is right and wrong. The general populaces give the press far too much authority. You believe if you see it on the news, it must be truth. So many in today's world take the news at face value. Yet there's so much more that you never read or hear about. People need to develop a constantly open mind to eliminate the possibility of being swayed by journalistic feeding frenzies based on what will increase ratings or sell more papers—entertainment—rather than uncovering the truth at all costs—education.

If individuals could learn to trust their own inner authority, a domino effect would be put into motion that could transform many areas, including government, press, religion, athletics, education and finance.

With the Internet, you have this problem magnified tenfold. Any ordinary human can create a reality, whether based on any sort of truth or not, and post it on the Internet. There, many people will believe it to be truth, merely because they read it on the Net. Not to mention the ability to openly view pornography, and how that affects the rate of development of children who view it.

Parents today are standing up to fight the infiltration of sexually explicit materials in American culture. This is nearly impossible, with the Internet available to so many children. Out of a need to not only monitor their use of the Internet, but also reduce their access to the pornography, laws will be enacted in the years ahead.

Part of why President Clinton's private life became such news was because, at light speed, details of his travails were in the hands of millions of people around the world. Do you think anyone would read transcripts from congressional sessions about where their money is going with such voracity? When was the last time the Internet carried, with such worldwide advertisement, the text of a bill that passed in Congress, or the peace proposals being written? Part of this cycle is hinged on the ordinary citizen's lack of creativity in their own personal lives. They look on, safely from their couch or office, and feed off of others' lives for their excitement. The American people have been conditioned to look at news as entertainment, instead of demanding moral value from journalism.

Boundaries need to become clear. If the Starr Report was a work of fiction, it would never have been able to get that kind of coverage. But the same sexually-explicit material, now deemed nonfiction and political, gets instantly into the hands of the children. Whether fiction or nonfiction, it still has the same effect on them. Americans need to see this reflection of lack of boundaries in themselves, and do something about it.

Q: What should we do?

JFK: You already see politicians grappling with how to handle the uncharted territory of this international cyberspace. It will take some time, but you'll begin to develop a monitoring system for the Internet, much like postal regulations and regulations for the public sale of sexual materials.

More importantly, teach your children to have rich, creative lives. Make sure they are properly stimulated, so they don't spend so much time on their computers or televisions. Nurture them creatively, get tools of expression into their hands, and teach them to be responsible for their own emotions.

As far as the Presidential scandal: Don't buy into the messages. Allow your president his privacy. Search within your own hearts for the places that perpetrate the same kind of lies you perceive him to be telling. Respect his private relationship with his wife. Honor her for the brave woman that she is.

I truly think President Clinton is going to have his best years directly after leaving office, when he will no longer be a public servant and can work as a private citizen to help change this system.

In retrospect, outside of the heated arguments of the moment, the world will come to see more and more how it was manipulated by media, politics and its own lack of creative expression. President Clinton will come out on top of this, and the world will learn the valuable lesson of privacy.

Q: In looking at government today, what do you think should be our major areas of focus? The country has been focused on a major sex scandal. What other areas should we be focused on?

JFK: One of the most important areas today which should be completely overhauled is how we finance education. Education has overtly fallen to the bottom of the list of political priorities. Yes, you hear many politicians talk about the need to increase money to provide adequate education, but in reality, the needs of big business have silently overtaken the needs of the children. Less and less funding for educating the children and more and more for sports arenas and shopping centers. Consider the amount of money private enterprise spends trying to sell children things: clothing, music, games, shoes. If all that money could miraculously be siphoned out of advertising, and into school programs, think of the power those schools would have.

The focus on commercialism goes hand in hand with the focus on the president's personal life. What is needed now is to move the attention away from the entertainment aspects of the private lives of famous people, and back into the hard work and difficult job of helping millions of the ordinary citizens, many living far below the poverty line, struggling to understand what is truly important.

Q: Do you think "Party of Twelve" is going to open people's eyes at all?

JFK: As you know, this group has been gathering and conversing for quite a long time. I entered the party shortly after my death only to find myself in quite credible company. I've watched as extraordinary people have joined this circle. The culmination of our work is about to be made known through this effort.

You must understand, and I don't mean this with any disrespect, but this book was not your idea.

Q: That's not surprising.

JFK: The party's agenda for this book is to cover as many aspects of culture as we can in order to give people a fuller, richer perspective of life on Earth, so that they may expand their awareness of their lives *before* they die. We also want to reflect how much power an individual, ordinary human being really has, despite what you are told by pop culture and entertainment journalism.

Each party member appeals to a different aspect of culture. Between all of us, we offer something for everyone. My expertise in the political arena is not just about my presidency and my life, I also speak for other great political leaders who have joined together to help bring about world peace.

Will we open people's eyes? Some, hopefully.

Q: I sense that this book will be controversial. That's exciting, because it sometimes take controversy to open people's eyes. It's frightening, though, that some people will consider this a form of blasphemy.

JFK: I understand fully what it's like to go against an established norm, particularly when you're challenging those who are in power. My mission in the White House was to open doors, not just to a higher understanding of politics, but to help the everyday men and women of this great country believe that they had influence in their political system. The changes that came about because of my presidency are still being felt today. But those changes were also what created the conspiracy against me.

Your position will be somewhat similar. With the book, we're trying to dismantle certain systems of power that have been in place a long time. You must, in the very least, be prepared to understand this. The difference is, you know that many are working with you and for you in order to bring about these changes as well, not just this party, but people all around the globe. We are all in this together.

Q: To move the conversation in another direction, I want to ask about Jackie. Is she in the same arena as you?

JFK: Yes, Jackie is here with me, working in this peace movement, but not in the political arena. As in our life together, we are still very connected.

Something that always interested me was the analogy of Camelot. If you recall, one of the primary plots in the story of Camelot was adultery. American people truly didn't know what they were saying when they were using that analogy! But even through all of that, Jackie remained a source of great strength.

She is perhaps the most intelligent woman I have ever known. Behind the closed doors of our life together, after a long day of tackling profound and sometimes international issues, her fresh perspective helped me to be the inspiring politician that I was.

Here in spirit, though she's not working in politics, she still advises me. She's more focused on helping the sick and suffering.

Q: Is Jackie there now? Could we speak to her?

Jackie Onassis: Yes.

Q: It's a pleasure to speak with you. Can you talk about what's happening in the world of publishing? Publishers have the power to shape people's minds, and yet they're doing celebrity "bios." Plus, we now know we can get information into people's hands overnight through the Internet, and yet publishing still takes twelve to eighteen months to get a book out.

JO: Publishing today is much like the changing politics of which Jack spoke. It's changed dramatically, even from a short time ago when I was an editor. So you forget how much of a time of change you're in. And we hope to be on the forefront of that change with this book.

As much as I was embraced as an editor, the truth was I was there for my love of books, and as a way for me to be connected to the world and still be sequestered. I didn't want the public life. The arena of publishing that I daily walked through was sheltering for and of me.

Publishing as I knew it is dying. Mergers are bringing the publishers and editors further out of touch with good writers, and moving the focus much more into entertainment. Books and movies are now married, often times the movie coming first. This union of East Coast publishing and West Coast entertainment has the capability of capturing the trends of the moment, but in the end, those books sell only in the moment they come out, during the trend. And not even then sometimes.

New publishing is comprised of smaller, savvy presses rising out of the shadows of the old guard. These presses have their distribution in place and can publish and distribute their own works within a certain sector of public buying power. With lower overhead, specific target markets and a closer connection to the reading public, they survive, and survive quite well.

For example, there is a publishing company in New York that survives solely on the sales of their beloved horticulture books. They provide high-quality books for those seeking information about gardening and flowers. They know their audience, and cater to its specific, sophisticated taste. They began because none of the larger houses saw a need for too terribly much information about flowers. But they are surviving well. The owners are more than comfortable, the employees are treated fairly and have room to work to find and develop new authors in this field. They aren't interested in following the trends of the moment. This growth in the smaller houses is very exciting. The ones who will rise to the top will know how to both follow the trends, and also put out books that will endure through those trends.

Another great change is print-on-demand. No longer will authors have to wait a year to see their work in print. Making these kinds of specialty services available to authors is also inspiring them to become their own independent publisher. They can now bypass a large publishing house, and have complete artistic control of their work, cover design, etc. These are exciting time in publishing.

Q: Can you give me some advice about this book?

JO: Remember your grace, and couple that with the confidence that you have a noble cause. The ability to put your best foot forward and trust the direction that you're going will be much more powerful for you than any spin or tag line that you can come up with.

This is a very noble project. You must project your knowledge of that nobility first and foremost. You know, in my life, I could walk into a room and people would be changed. I don't believe I was that powerful, but the aura of who I was, the legendary status that surrounded me allowed my presence in a room to leave an indelible mark upon the people who saw me.

I do believe I possessed a gift of grace, a gift of the knowledge of myself, partly through my destiny, partly through my family, and partly through being thrust at such a young age into the public eye. Being in a position of destiny, Jack and I were changing the world. We were bringing about a great awareness. We were very idealistic and we believed in our idealism. We loved our naiveté, even through the difficulty in our marriage and the personal challenges we went through. We were somehow able to hang onto the ordinary people that we were and the naiveté of those ordinary people. Through the grace of God and the people that I chose to surround myself with, I was able to pass onto our children this sense of grace and inner identity. I taught them how to surround themselves with people who understand who they really are.

This is what you must do. You must retain your naiveté and become the knowledge that you want to pass on, knowing that you're tackling great Goliaths, knowing also that there probably will be a backlash from culture. People will try to tell you that your naiveté is foolish. Believe me, in the difficult times of our marriage, when I was in the public eye with young children and the pressure to be perfect, there were a lot of people in Jack's circle who thought that my innocence and my choice to remain naive would be his downfall.

But now, being able to see from a much higher perspective, I would tell you to err on the side of naiveté. Surround yourself with trusted, grounded, compassionate friends who will help be your barometer in those times when your naiveté is being tested.

ALBERT Einstein

March 14, 1879 ~ April 18, 1955

Reincarnation, Education & Gravity

Q: It couldn't be any more appropriate, what with the thunderstorm outside, that we're here today to talk to Albert Einstein.

AE: First, I'd like to say, it's a very great honor to be able to speak in this way. I have been working for quite some time to make this all come about. Understand, this is the first time I've been able to explain my points of view so clearly and articulate what I've learned since my death. Thank you, thank you very much!

In my youth, I was considered to be an idiot by some people. Today I am considered a genius. The world is still again going through this. Geniuses are being called idiots because they are challenging the way life is perceived. It's really no accident that we have created this opportunity to be able to speak through you and bring some new light to some of old concepts. But be careful! You, too, will be called idiots!

Q: Mr. Einstein...

AE: Oh please, call me Albert!

Q: Okay, Albert, the first area we'd like to discuss is reincarnation. We had a conversation recently about why you haven't reincarnated. What can you tell us about that?

AE: Understand, during the late 1800s and early 1900s, scientists were more spiritually-based than they are now. When I say "spiritual," I'm not referring to a religious experience or a belief system, but instead I'm referring to energy, and the quest to get past the very smallest particles of matter and into the space between the particles, into the consciousness of the particles. During the time I was receiving the information about relativity, I was unearthing the essence of so many aspects of life on that molecular level. Even with that, I could only begin to touch that space while I was alive. So reincarnation was a topic that I never really had a chance to explore.

Now, coming into the new millennium from this place of pure spirit, it doesn't seem at all unlikely that I would be given a chance to speak directly from Afterlife to continue to expound upon the theories of relativity and the basis of matter. And from here, I have an entirely new perspective on reincarnation.

When I first talked about relativity, I was talking about the relationship of time and space. I was talking about a particular set of contained guidelines that rule physical matter. This says nothing about what exists outside of physical matter, in the space between matter. There were a great many who believed at the time that nothing existed outside the realm of physical matter. Physical matter was believed to be the primary reality. Many of you have come to believe over the years that physical matter is really the secondary reality. It's the manifestation of thought, the by-product of something that exists outside of time and space.

Now as I speak of reincarnation, think differently. Don't think just of your human being self sitting in a chair, but think of what is at the root of that physical being that sits in the chair, the invisible spirit that is contained within the thoughts, between the particles that is the intelligence behind the creation of matter. When you look beyond matter as the primary source, you begin to see in this invisible world of spirit a great deal of unexplainable phenomenon.

Here, in the condition that I exist in now, I'm able to be everywhere at once. I'm able to be talking to you here, while at the same time, I can be working with scientists who are studying regeneration on a molecular level. I can also be working with feeding the hungry children. I can be doing so many things at one time because I can be everywhere.

You might say, "How can that be?" It's hard for the human mind to comprehend that kind of reach. But just think about gravity. It's everywhere at once, at work everywhere all over the world. For the most part, it's the same kind of condition in Afterlife.

Looking at reincarnation with the human mind, it's easier to comprehend from a linear time frame. You're thinking of the me, Einstein, who lived during the first part of the twentieth century. Then, the me, Einstein, died. Time passed, and you think reincarnation could now have taken place, a little farther down the timeline. If that were the case, I would be born into a new life to be a new person who could quite possibly be living today. That's the perspective of reincarnation from the human mind.

From the perspective of spirit, the inner gravity that brings together a human life and surges through the space between the particles is outside the realm of the time-space relationship. Linear time simply does not exist from the perspective of gravity. Spirit has its roots outside time and space. Perhaps you might determine that root or center to be something called God. From the root of reality comes the primary function to recreate life, in one form or another. That is simply the very nature of this life-giving energy: regeneration. Energy, by its very nature, regenerates itself.

From a scientific point of view, God is much like a black hole, devoid of time and space. From the spiritual perspective, God is all there is. That is the paradox. And this is why both science and spirit need to be present to create a complete picture of reality. And also why humans need to learn to live within the truth of this paradox, in all metaphorical layers.

The origins of the consciousness of Barbara With can be traced back into the great gestalt of all possibility, into the mind of God. As you trace your origins back to the source, back to the root, past the three-dimensional reality and into the invisible substance that is the electricity of your spirit, you find everything inside you, and yet, outside the laws of time and space. Everything that exists comes from that intersection of all realities, and you have a piece of that everything inside you. You share that piece with every other living human being on the planet. All life springs from this same nothingness. It is from this root that all your reincarnated lives spring, independent of time, therefore all taking place simultaneously, like gravity.

Reincarnation is not necessarily just a matter of, for example, having a life in 1845 as a businessman in London, then dying, and now in 1998 living as a literary agent in New York City, as if those lives are separated from one another by time (1845 to 1998) and space (London to New York). Reincarnation is instead a present- moment reality that is your personal connection through your spirit to the part of you that is that regenerating energy of what you might call God. As a human, I believe you could, with proper training and experimentation, learn to perceive all your lives being lived simultaneously. Theoretically, you should be able to retrain your perception to look from the space between the molecules and experience all lives at once. This would seem a natural step in the evolution of the human consciousness.

Because the source is outside the realm of time and space, and you have access to all there is, you can actually, if you so choose, live this same life, as Barbara With, over and over again for all eternity. In reliving this life, you could experience the infinite possibilities for how things could possibly play out. And believe me, with the number of decisions that you make in a lifetime, the possibilities are limitless as to how your life would be different from one pass to the next.

For example, one infinite possibility for Tina "reincarnating" into this life leads her to be a mildly successful literary agent, divorced with three children who ends up remarrying a rich man from the Hampton's. She gives up her agency and finishes her life giving cocktail parties and watching her children go to expensive prep schools. That is only one of the infinite possibilities that exist for her to reincarnate into this life over and over again.

This is the fun of life. This is the joyfulness of the experience of human life. And this, for me, is what reincarnation is all about.

So what about that in businessman London in the 1800s? It's no longer a timeline. It's no longer a linear manifestation. It's part of the bigger process that allows you the power to tap into areas between the matter. Understand, reincarnation isn't necessarily about several different lives that you're creating. In that sense, when you utilize the process of tapping into your source energy, you find you are also a part of every human being that lives on the planet. You have access to everyone else's knowledge because you have that intersection of what you call God where all knowledge and all possibility and the greatest of the greatest creations exist. You have access to all information of the universe. I did try to say this in my life, that there was a great deal more information that can be tapped into.

I can go back into my life as Einstein and create what you might call a parallel universe, wherein I didn't do so poorly in school, but also maybe I didn't come up with the theory of relativity. In the parallel universe, the theory of relativity exists in the great gestalt of information and someone else picks up on it and brings it through. I wasn't responsible for creating the Theory of Relativity. Don't think that without me, it never would have happened. I was just the manifestation of how it was going to happen in that life.

Q: Is it possible that intelligence is simply one's ability to access the information that is readily available?

AE: Yes, yes, oh my yes. The truth is that all information, all ideas, everything that could possibly exist, is accessible from within the human being, most specifically, through the use of the human mind. The human mind is trained from the time it comes onto the planet to look outside itself for answers. You're taught to rely on what people tell you and how they define the world. Luckily, the artists and scientists are people who must see for themselves! But they are so often then labeled as outsiders, or off base, or even nuts.

I had a bit of denial built into my personality. I found it amusing that people thought I was crazy and wacky. But I knew I knew what I knew. I knew how to tap into a profound source of information. The greater purpose for doing poorly in school was to set the world up to understand that this vast knowledge did not really come from me, Einstein the person. I was merely the human conduit.

I certainly was gifted with the knowledge of how to tap into these areas. You're now on the verge of coming to understand that truth. How lucky the world is to have exceptional explorers like yourselves to forget the dictates of society, step outside the expectations and take a chance to see what indeed you can tap into!

What you're finding out is, not only can you access all the knowledge from within, but it's an everyday occurrence. It can happen at the kitchen table or sitting on the floor in the bathroom. You can tap into the knowledge at any time and any place. This is indeed a time of great expansion and exploration.

Q: If we can bring this message to the world, and if they start believing it, then can we overhaul the education system in America to be much more helpful to children?

AE: Oh, my, my, yes! Educational systems throughout the world are undergoing so much change. You're not really capable, from your three-dimensional, time-based reality, of seeing how long it will take the changes to take hold. You'll start finding, through educational experimentation, teaching methods that aren't about feeding children information and hoping that they will retain it. It will be about helping them tap into the parts of themselves that are personally connected to their piece of all that knowledge. It will be about training the children to look within.

It's not that teachers become obsolete, it's that they become a much different kind of guide for the children. In the not-too-distant future, more and more of this kind of education will become available. Certain children will be subjected to training to find the source within themselves, to tap into the other 90% of their brains, into these areas of the mind of God, if you will, and bring back the information into the three-dimensional world. You'll find that children will register on I.Q. tests very high, even though they might not have been given that information through a three-dimensional source.

The possibilities are very exciting and revolutionary at this stage of development.

Q: At this point, keeping an eye towards education and helping a child succeed in this society, what do you think are the most important aspects of the parent/child relationship?

AE: This goes back to the questions of nurturing. What does nurturing actually mean? Unfortunately, in your society, nurturing has come to mean convenience for the parents. To nurture your children to do what you say or to be what you want somehow conforms to a set of ideals that will make your life easier. I hate to be so blunt about this condition, but it's part of what is undermining some of the cultural morality. Not that every parent is so selfish, but there's an unconscious trend of parents to raise their children in this way.

One important change is coming from those parents who can learn to parent themselves. In other words, parents who look within themselves and bring balance through integration of their own lives will teach their children, through example, how to take care of themselves. As it is now, many parents project their own fear, reactions and thoughts onto their children, and then try to take care of their own feelings through their kids. It's a roundabout way to parent, and affects the children more than you know. Those parents who take complete responsibility for their own nurturing won't need to live their lives through their children. They will teach their children how to be themselves, not what they, as parents, want the children to be. That's really the important aspect of this change.

The beautiful part about this is that it forces the parent to take responsibility for their own feelings about what they want their children to do but aren't willing to do for themselves. A classic example is, perhaps you feel a need for your child to learn to play the piano. It's very important for you to have your child play, so you hire a great piano teacher. You force your child to sit down every day and practice. Truthfully, your child has no interest in playing the piano. But for some reason, you deem it important that this child sits at the piano and learns to play. He would like to be out playing baseball. But you see no redeemable future and no aesthetic quality in baseball, so you put the child into the box that you think is best for him.

In a more evolved society, children would be nurtured to explore how to let their own inner life come to the surface and then manifest their inner life in their activities and actions. In other words, the child would be allowed to go play baseball, and the parent would take the piano lessons. This would be one of the most beneficial changes in perception for parents to understand.

Q: It seems like right now it's in vogue for parents to come up with labels for their child's differences, for example, ADD and autism and various other things that parents believe are some sort of weakness.

AE: Yes, this is again the parenting of the parent. The parents want to fit their own perceptions into a box that will be easily understandable to their limited intellectual capabilities. Creating these labels is a function of a dysfunctional culture. The term "ADD" is for the parents. In other cultures, children with what you might label "Attention Deficit Disorder" were dealt with much differently.

Take Native American culture. There, if children displayed the traits of "ADD," the answer was to let them run around outside all day. A simple answer. Then they came in and were tired. In that culture, there were many mothers. It was quite the example of good community. Mother didn't have to clean up the teepee and cook all the meals until Father came home from hunting. It was a collective. When it was time to skin the buffalo, there were five, six, seven women sitting around that buffalo, preparing the meat and having a good time. All of their children were around them in an outer circle, taking care of each other. When one of the children fell and got hurt, it wasn't necessarily the birth mother who leapt up. And it wasn't an issue of, "My child needs to behave well so that I appear to be a good mother." That was nonsense in that culture.

Also, the Native American people did not make their children sit still in incremental hourly segments and focus on words on a page or a blackboard. They allowed their children to live free under the sky, the sun and the moon, to listen to the rhythm of Mother Earth's heartbeat. Today, everyone is expected to have the same bodily rhythm: Nine-to-Five. Now scientists are discovering this internal clock, and how important it is for each human to attune themselves to their own clock.

It's astounding how many labels there are, too, more and more every day. Once you begin to attack these "illnesses" with these multiple labels by treating the parent, you can then train the parent how to nurture the child that seemingly doesn't fit into culture. Now you're changing culture.

Q: Let's talk about serious diseases, like cancer and spinal cord injuries. Can the body really heal itself? Can you give us your insight into what serious illness is?

AE: Yes, it's true that the body, on a very elemental level, has been programmed to be a regenerative vehicle. When you have a simple cut on your hand, you wash the wound and put on a bandage. After about a week and a half, it's gone. You haven't been thinking for a week and a half, "Please heal this wound." It heals as a function of a molecular command. Your body, by its own nature, is designed to keep itself functioning and regenerating.

But understand: bringing spirit into physical form creates a conflict. You've now introduced a mechanism programmed for regeneration into the matrix of a world that is, by its own design, degenerative, and meant to challenge the programs of regeneration with different levels of illness. This is not unnatural within the laws of nature. But from a spiritual level, you, as scientists, are learning about the capabilities of your physical body and what it can do for itself, how it can regenerate by tapping into the space between the particles and accessing information.

It's difficult to understand illness fully, because you don't have a lot of information through the course of human history. You don't know if cancer existed 1,500 years ago and was called something else. In this day and age it's cancer; then, it was much more mysterious, defined within the realm of the culture in which it appeared. It might have been interpreted as the revenge of an angry god because the crops weren't planted on time.

There are complex structures within culture that influence the body's ability to regenerate. It's not just an isolated function of the body. It's very connected to what's happening within the environment around it, and also to the openness of the intellect and the emotions of the recipient of the physical body.

You have made great strides in healing some very deadly diseases. If you look back over the course of medical history, in the past 100 years there have been great advances to saving lives and helping people live longer. People often died at the turn of the century because of minor afflictions that science and medicine have since discovered how to cure.

Now you are on a new frontier. You're being challenged to go past just what medical science has taught you. You are once again returning to the idea that you can heal yourself. You've experienced the regenerative, i.e. healed wounds, mended hearts, miracles, even as you experience all of the degeneration as well. Living with those two energy matrices at once often times results in a malfunctioning of the physical body.

This doesn't imply you can just think away all your illnesses. You must integrate all aspects of your being. To do this, you must study and experiment with the workings of your entire self: your intellect in relation to your emotions, in relation to your intuitions, in relation to your spirit, in relation to the environment, all in present moment. You must find new ways to make this duality work together and for each other.

As you move forward in this great progression of discovery, many will have the capability to do miraculous things with their bodies, without the help of medical science. These are indeed exciting times.

So, yes, in answer to the question, your body is meant to be regenerative, and you are being challenged to find the answers within to facilitate that natural regeneration.

Q: It's been made clear that it wasn't our decision to do this book, instead you found us. I've heard that you received the theory of relativity in a dream. Was it given to you in that way?

AE: Oh, my, yes! There is really no one human being that is responsible for any great amount of knowledge. I was only responsible in the sense that I didn't wake up from my dream and say that I was crazy and not speak up about it. I was responsible for the knowledge in that I made a decision to pass that knowledge along and carry the information into the three-dimensional world.

You are conduits for the manifestation of matter and

intelligence on the planet. This is really the process for attaining all knowledge. The beautiful part is that you have free will to choose the information you're going to channel onto the planet. But consider this: I delivered my message successfully, and yet, understand, I also unknowingly gave the world a key for its possible complete degeneration.

Q: What was it like growing up as Albert Einstein? Did you have these kinds of mystical experiences often?

AE: I was born into a family where I got just enough love and nurturing, just enough freedom and a great deal of humor. Life was very funny to me, sort of whimsical. And yes, even as a child, I had a sense of being tapped into a greater source of knowledge and energy. I often felt crazy, out of touch, but carefree and unfettered by the confines of conventional thinking.

As a child, I had very vivid dreams. Many a morning I would sit with my mother and relate to her the dramas of the night before. While she could allow me the room to talk about my dreams, I dare say she felt like she had a crazy child on her hands most of the time.

I was also nearly impossible to discipline. My mother used to tell me, if I hadn't been so naturally good-humored, she might have lost her mind raising me!

Later on, as a "rational" adult, I went deeper into the science of the infrastructure of the universe than anyone ever had before. Imagine the dissent around me, from the scientific community! Luckily, there was group of us that supported each other's explorations in those depths. I faced the dissention head-on with the very knowledge I was tapping into. Not that I wasn't plagued with doubts sometimes. I got very depressed. In fact, I went through a period of being quite downtrodden about the human condition in the world, about this insanity I felt. But looking back on those times, I see that those times of depression were meant to be times of rest. I didn't realize what it meant to be this conduit for knowledge in this way, nor the implications that it had on my physical body. Bringing information in from a source outside the physical world, outside of time and space and still from within myself created a bit of a strain on my body. When I brought that knowledge into the physical, it had a direct affect on my molecules.

I slept a lot through different periods of my life. That's what happened to me. I disguised my need to rest in a form of depression.

But each and every person channels knowledge, information, creative ideas, artistic expressions into the world every day. But without your consent to open yourself up and consciously participate in the process of the creative effort, all of that mystery and knowledge remains unseen and untapped.

Q: So had we been too afraid of what people might think, this book would never come out. But because we're willing to take the chance, we're going to be able to deliver this information.

AE: That is correct. That's why there was a great selection process on our part of possible avenues through which we could manifest this book into the three-dimensional form. There were lots of different ideas. There was talk of working with the manipulation of matter in such a way that we would create a manuscript that would just be found somewhere. That would be a lot less controversial.

The controversy you're going to create is part of what will spur people on to think about themselves in different ways, to explore different possibilities of understanding the self and relationships to other people. In this way, putting out this book of ours fulfills the most pressing need we have here in the Afterlife: to help to bring about world peace.

Q: We've been talking a lot about world peace with each member of the party. Our consensus is that world peace starts within the individual. Can you share your thoughts with us on that?

AE: The pursuits of my life were about expressing some fairly revolutionary information that made people think differently about the structure of the universe and the nature of reality. This information is not necessarily irrelevant to me now that I'm in the Afterlife. Don't give up your pursuit of knowledge about the nature of physical, three-dimensional reality. There is always more to learn.

We just feel, from this place of spirit, it's much more important now to influence and inspire you to find ways to live together. Look at all the different perspectives, like we used to do when we were young. My circle of friends would get together, have a beer and toss around some outrageous idea. You, as a human race, must learn to work together.

It's much more important for the world to find a way to work together than it is to find a particular gem of information or a nugget of knowledge or the next great scientific discovery. Without the love that passes between you as humans, without cooperation and self-respect, you will live in a very segregated, turbulent world.

All of us here have been in positions of notoriety and power, each in our own way, perhaps more intensely than the average person. We achieved a kind of recognition and social standing that allowed us to speak from our soapbox, to make a difference in a broader intellectual sense. And now, in the Afterlife, we are still learning new and clever ways to work with each other and with you.

Q: About our ability to work together: How will we be able to integrate the spiritual side of healing with what goes on in the hospitals and labs? We had a recent discussion about molecular cell regeneration and wondered, is the answer raising money for more research in the lab, or getting out of that box and looking within?

AE: The answer is really a combination of both. The advances that medical science has made over this past century have been truly miraculous. There are many people alive today because of that research, because of the frontier of young doctors excited by the prospect of uncovering new answers to cures for what were formerly deadly diseases. That area has been miraculous, in and of itself.

Individuals within the area of research are going to broaden their personal perspectives to be more inclusive of other possibilities. Still, you will get a great deal of resistance from the medical research community. Not because they don't want to find a way to regeneration. They've poured their lives and time and energy into their work. They've discovered a great many cures, and answers to prolonging life and relieving misery. Their resistance isn't about not wanting to find those cures. Their resistance tells them that life is not constructed in this way, *because* of what they've seen, because of the damage to the physical body they've experienced. Many cannot conceive that internally-fueled cell regeneration is possible. That's where the changes will have to take place. I don't want them to abandon their work. I want them to be more inclusive in their work.

As you yourselves have said, you're coming up against a very strong political system. This system says you have to be dependent upon someone else for your well-being, your doctor, instead of trusting your body to tell you what it needs, thereby developing clear channels within your body and a confidence and firsthand knowledge about your body.

That might mean that you have a clear channel into your physical body and you can tell there's something wrong in your menstrual cycle and in your womb, so then you can go to a medical doctor and get help finding the cure. There is a great force in this culture to take away that self-authority and self-knowledge. It says, "You can't possibly know that about your body because you're not a doctor."

There's a power structure of politics in the high finance that medical science has become. You see that they've raised billions and billions of dollars within the medical research community to find the cure for AIDS. And yet, when they do come up with the experimental cure, the cost is so outrageous that it's prohibitive for the ordinary human being with AIDS to be able to participate in this kind of research or have any hope of getting that kind of help.

It's the people with the diseases who don't have access to these new, expensive treatments who are being forced to look into alternative possibilities. They are the ones who are spearheading the movement. Out of that movement is coming a consciousness about self-regeneration. Out of that will come a conflict with the political system that creates the drugs that then make a huge profit for the corporations. This is an area that needs to be explored and uncovered.

You're going up against many layers of culture here, many layers of fear.

Q: I don't want this next question to sound flip, but we're sitting here talking to people who are so-called "dead" and you're fine. What difference does it make, since we're going to die anyway? Is it our job as humans to try and stay alive?

AE: Now you sound like a teenager who says, "Since I'm getting out of school anyway, what's the difference if I flunk or graduate? I don't want to go on to college, so why should I strive and learn?"

The goal is not necessarily that you have to make the honor roll. You are all scientists. You came here to learn. The idea is, while you're passing through your life, participate fully. Be here in present moment, fully, creatively, emotionally. Live in the joy of the miracle of being alive, with the anticipation that you're making a difference for your children and their children and their children.

Being human is very real and very important. You aren't *just* physical beings, but you certainly *are* physical beings. You have a body now. I don't. But it's not the end result that's so important, it's the journey, you see, that you don't want to miss.

But let me assure you, you can lose your physical

body, and still have an attitude!

Q: So it's our job to live happily and explore?

AE: Yes yes yes!!

Adolph HITLER

April 20, 1889 ~ April 30, 1945

Karma, Hell & Destiny

Q: May I call you Adolph?

AH: Yes, that's fine.

Q: I want to ask you first, why did you come to speak to us?

AH: Are you certain this is the question? Would it be more appropriate for me to ask you, why did you come to speak to me? I am quite sure many people are wondering why you are talking to me.

For me, I know that nothing I could say, to anyone, could ever undo the evil that happened around my life and those times. But it is vitally important for me to apologize. Does that sound impossible?

Q: My first reaction is why?

AH: To begin with, let's get a few things straight. There are two parts to my story. There is the human side, and then there is the energetic side of what happened. To fully understand, at first these two parts need to be viewed separately.

I choose to start with the human side. In this case, I apologize for the lifetimes of suffering, for all of the pain of all of the people, all the uncounted people—and there were so many more than anyone will ever really know— who went through an actual living hell on Earth imposed upon them by this outside, evil force of the holocaust. This is an ungodly thing we are talking about.

I was the center of this maelstrom. I was the center of the vortex of energy that had been set in motion thousands of year before it actually happened.

But that is an energetic idea. I digress.

[Several moment of silence...]

It's difficult for me to separate the human side and the energetic side, but I will try, for the sake of this interview.

[More silence...]

In answer to your question, "Why," perhaps there can be a sort of redemption if I confess to these human crimes, seek atonement or at the very least, tell you that I accept the consequences of this burning karma I have brought upon myself, and articulate this experience, for the sake of perhaps being able to integrate into totality the two sides to this story.

You see, everyone remembers me as a force, a symbol, if you will, of the worst case scenario for being a human. My being has become a universal force, if you will, associated with pure hate.

Q: You have become the metaphor for evil.

AH: Believe me, my reign reached to all corners of the globe, to every corner of the planet, and even through time. But these executions, this destruction must somehow be stopped.

Yes, yes, I know, this coming from, well, it's laughable, isn't it...but, from Hitler. You think, who is *Hitler* to say this must stop NOW?

Why didn't this Hitler stop it THEN? Now, that is the energetic tale, much different from the compassion of the human suffering. This side of the story also must be told. But it must not be told in any way that takes away from the truth of that suffering. This is why I have agreed to speak.

Q: Are you saying that you had to show us what we are capable of doing to each other?

AH: I am saying I showed you what could and does happen, to the Nth degree, within a human condition when it is so devoid of emotion that there is an absolute vacuum of existence. I chose to be the personification of the darkest force of nature because it was needed, but not to teach you to learn to live in peace. That will merely be a by-product, eventually.

I am the expression of the depths of your own possibilities. You need to know this of yourselves. Not to judge and punish, but to embrace with intention to transform, to then fill the void with worth again. To do that, someone had to carry the reality of that darkness into the physical world, to challenge human spirit to rise again out of its own dual nature.

I knew, from a place of spirit, what I was getting myself into before I came. Much like Albert, I had a system of denial in place in order to do my job effectively. And much like Albert, I received information through inner voices and dreams.

Q: But what was your mind telling you when you were here on Earth about what you were doing?

AH: My mind? My conscious mind had been wounded from the time I was very young. I cannot describe to you the atrocities I witnessed as my father became the dictator of my childhood, and threatened the very existence of the only person I thought could protect me, my mother. She was the source of all life for me, and she loved me as if I were Jesus, as if I had come here for a special mission.

My mother was quite connected to spirit herself, but she was young and lacking in self-esteem when she met my father. We children became her only reason for living. She needed to be there to protect us. After losing my brother in death at such an early age, she felt she failed in her "raison d'etre" and fell to illness.

Q: Were you abused as a child?

AH: Child abuse surely was the basis for the human root of the psychosis from which I suffered. My father would scald me with hot water as a baby, burn me and threaten that if I didn't behave he would put me in the wood stove. I do not believe he would have gone so far, but the imagination of a child makes many things real.

There were other, more atrocious things he did that I don't wish to speak of. But the effect of losing my childhood innocence and the harsh dichotomy of my parents twisted my young mind into a place of complete lack of any connection to any inner feeling about myself other than self-loathing and contempt. I was dragged through the mud of sexual abuse as well, and by the time I reached puberty, I could find no internal motivation to produce any accomplishment.

Yes, it was true I had an interest in art, but it was the artist's lifestyle that attracted me, the ability to be so slovenly and unregulated. Oh, yes, I enjoyed the drawing, to a degree, but I was not very good at it, and my rejection from school was only another move on the game board of my destiny, to push me farther away from the light.

So I, with no light within, and no self-worth, was rejected, kicked around, experimenting with sadomasochism and drugs, living a life of degeneracy. I was prime material for the military in Germany at that time.

As I dove deeper and deeper into my own absence of self, I found no alternative but to project that out over the external world. The Jews became metaphors for my own idea of the filth I possessed so deeply within me that could only be routed out by complete extermination. Because I could not conceive with my conscious mind that these feelings were about me, I grew farther and farther away from reality, casting my deepest hatred outside myself and fluctuating between hatred of the Jews and thoughts of suicide.

Now, here I was, finally being motivated as I joined the military. Suddenly, I had a cultural support system for externalizing my self-hatred. In this I thrived. Where before I was noxious about my body habits, I became obsessively clean. I was fighting for my Motherland, as a way to somehow make good the life of suffering my own mother lived.

After the fall of Germany during World War I, I was myself defeated. I went into a seclusion, where I could not eat or talk or listen to anything. Just as my mother condemned herself for the death of my brother, I condemned myself for the defeat of all of Germany, and the hatred grew.

The voices within my head were telling me that I was the one who had to do something about this utter lack of life within Germany at this time. I was the one who was going to lead the German people to their resurrection. But with each step I took, I stepped farther and farther away from any life that may have existed in the desert within. To each new level of power I climbed, there arose even deeper, more insatiable fears that needed even more externalizing.

By the time I had arrived at the top of the empire, I was completely void of emotions other than fear and rage. Do you think this was hell on Earth? I tell you it was.

Q: Why did you experiment on humans?

AH: I thought a lot about life from molecular levels. In this way, my thoughts were much more like Albert's than Faust's. Those experiments were about human waste. In my mind, I truly believed I was saving the world, or trying to save the world from human waste. I was hoping to create a purity within the molecular systems.

Q: A purity of what?

AH: Of ethics, of molecules, of connections. After Germany's defeat, I found myself pondering if the evil, vacuous emptiness of my life was genetic in origin. When a person lacks so much inner substance, there are natural thoughts about finding inherent flaws within the mechanism.

Isn't it ironic, because I was a walking void of emotions, I manifested that void everywhere I went.

Q: You said there is an energetic side to the story, and that we have to keep them separated. What is that side, and why do they have to be separated?

AH: The separation is necessary to assure that you do not allow the energetic side to this story to trick you into thinking that because it was part of a larger plan that I am not being held responsible for my actions. Both sides of the paradox of this event must be examined thoroughly to understand the meaning.

Q: And could you define exactly what you mean when you say the "energetic" side?

AH: That is merely looking at what happened from a scientific perspective, using no judgment or moral indicators, no preconceived discernment about what the events meant. The human side examines those things from a place of deep anguish and human compassion. The energetic side examines those things as nature.

From an energetic perspective, before I was born into Adolph Hitler, there was an energy building around the Earth. This energy was filled with imbalances from the over-weighted posture of meaningless power.

The consciousness of developing humans took the lessons of a greater God and used them to create even more victimization for themselves. Jesus' followers removed the focus from believing in themselves as reflections of God, as he was, and turned the focus outward, to him as a redeemer. The Islamic believers took the words of Allah and began to separate themselves from one another into sects, using those words violently against each other. The Jews had forever been victims, persecuted from the beginning of their known time. Along with all these individual interpretations of God came possibilities of Satan as well.

There were many discussions about how this would manifest. Those in spirit knew that in order to balance the energy of a God-consciousness that was representing the collective good, there would also be a manifestation in physical form of the absence of good. The end goal being completely balancing the two.

Think energetically, purely energetically. Don't look with a human heart now. One rule of the Universe says that for every action, there is an equal and opposite reaction. Jesus brought to the planet the physical manifestation of all that was good. The only way to bring a balance in spirit, over the long term of the planet, was to manifest into form this absence of good. In fact, the absence of anything. And yet how to physicalize nothingness?

A large group of souls came together and trained to be participants in this movement. The souls of all who were victims of the holocaust understood that, by undergoing this experiment for the greater good, they might have to come through hell on Earth. The promise was that, because they were all participating together, the rapid and extremely emotional exit they would make from the planet would bond them together in such a way that the strength of their power would be solidified into pure compassion and balance would be restored.

It was a difficult decision on *all* parties involved. We all knew we would be in hell, at one point in the process or another.

Q: You're saying, it was a dance in which everyone participated, even those today still dealing with the healing of the holocaust.

AH: Yes, those souls that incarnated as the Jews and the Gypsies, the gays and the handicapped, and all the people merely caught in the crossfire, all those souls spoke together about the possibility of bringing balance back to the consciousness.

These were grave discussions. We were all very serious. We knew we were working for something far different than what would be perceived. I knew, before I was born, that I would be "going to hell" if I chose this life. I accepted the assignment. If it hadn't been me, it would have been someone else.

But yes, I must take full responsibility for my human influence. I knew what was going to happen, yet, just as a child does not know what he is really wishing for, I was not prepared for hell in this way. If life as Adolph Hitler was not hellish enough, what happened to me after my death certainly has been. I have suffered, perhaps equally to any of those who suffered under my reign. The hell that burns within me is reciprocal to the hell I caused on Earth.

But, as I said, to those who ask my human side about the complete absence of compassion as a human being, I have no response.

Q: Why did you choose suicide?

AH: At the end, when I was in the last hours of life, I started hallucinating the reflection of the deep psychoses that made up the place where my emotions were supposed to be. There was no other way for me to escape from the destiny of my own void. I had to be the one to execute myself. There was no one else qualified.

Q: My husband's mother lost her brother when you invaded Poland. Can you tell us about that first act of rage? Why Warsaw?

AH: Poland was a stepping stone, a way for me to flex my powers of manifestation. It was a solidification for me of how far my influence within my own ranks would reach. Poland had traditionally been a country set adrift. From as far back as most of recorded time, she has given away her infrastructure. Militarily, she was a weak link.

But energetically, Poland would launch the start of the systematic breakdown of social structure within the hearts of all men.

Albert had just introduced the idea of relativity onto the planet through his dreams and his advanced understanding of spirit on a molecular level. The arrival of that information pulled a rug out from under the scientific community. Its mere presence opened and closed minds very quickly, galvanizing a segment of culture into chaos and uncertainty.

At the same time, Sigmund was presenting similarly upsetting ideas in the area of sex, the mind and psychology. We were a people who did not know who we were anymore, from the ground up: molecularly, intellectually, emotionally after the loss of the war. A great force was setting society up to receive me and my inflated projection over humanity. You really must see the holocaust was no accident.

And yet, who am I to ask you to see the divine planning in something that created hell on Earth? That in itself might seem atrocious to some.

Q: Are you in hell now?

AH: Yes.

Q: What's it like?

AH: It's torment, as if my insides are burning. I cannot lose consciousness and I am dominated by the spirits of every one of the people that were taken and all the spirits of their families. They have been given the power to deal as they will with my soul.

Q: But if they chose that life for themselves, why do they get to blame you and hold you up for it?

AH: Let's speak of an average case. Have you ever felt like you wanted to kill someone? Seriously, have you ever felt the rage of wanting to even hurt someone?

Q: Yes.

AH: So you have chosen to come here, knowing what your life will be like, and accepting the consequences of what you are about to do. You bring with you an agenda. Does your wanting someone hurt diminish in any way from the experience of the essential part of you, the spirit part of you?

Q: No.

AH: No, indeed, more, it *is* the essential part of you, what you came here to accomplish. Yet, you still have to be accountable for how that energy of anger and rage manifests onto the planet. You still create for yourself your own karma about your actions that you must eventually experience.

The human side can't see the whole picture, the one spirit is capable of perceiving. In this separated state, people get hurt. In the process of waking up to the entirety of your nature, you are hurt. You are hurt to remember what you were supposed to know, you are hurt to see the infractions you commit upon yourself in your amnesia of evolution.

You simply have to feel the human experience in order to rearrange the long-term evolution of the human. Being fine in spirit does not necessarily equal being fine as a human.

Q: Is this karma?

AH: Yes, this is my karma, to burn off the illusions that my human mind created while in life on Earth to bring an energetic balance back to my soul. I knew, before entering into that life, that I would experience this burning. I chose to take on the imbalance of human consciousness, and essentially take the world to hell, just as Jesus tried to bring the world to heaven, in order to obtain balance.

For me, I must have had a deep desire for such solitude to have come to life as this man in the 20th century, for now I am alone. Even amongst this party, there has been no one in my world except the haunted terror of my actions for what seems like eternity.

Do you think that even this devil, this manifestation of what so many see as Satan, can be healed, for the sake of the greater good? This is going to be quite controversial. Are you aware of this? That Jesus has forgiven Adolph Hitler?

And what will your world have if Hitler is forgiven? What if I told you that some of the souls of those who died have already forgiven me? That alone is a major opening. It has been their forgiveness that has filled that emotional void within my being, slowly, not taking me from this hell, mind you. I tortured a nation as a reflection of a torture within. Yet, the collective consciousness of those souls needs to forgive me, for their own karma and to complete this experiment to balance spirit.

Q: We talked to Einstein about reincarnation, about the infinite possibilities of life.

AH: Good man, Albert.

Q: Are you coming back to reincarnate or are you living all these infinite possibilities from where you are?

AH: I am not only living all the infinite possibilities, but I am living all the possibilities of all the souls of those humans that I took out, on a multidimensional chess board. Yes, there are other lives of Adolph Hitler. Did you know the one where I save the world? Where it all works out? The only problem is, imagine that.

Your karma is the return on your actions. It's so strong that you can create one life that shines for no reason other than you are in the right place at the right time. In your other lives, you may live your dismal possibility of life in a loveless marriage, or even something worse, like the death of a child or being Hitler himself. Whatever the details, the karma returns to balance you.

What I did, on an energetic level, was part of a long-term plan of destiny and karma to integrate the duality that had become too strongly rooted on Earth. Since they experienced that energy of the holocaust, the "victims" are now fused together, all those twelve million spirits. They are now one powerful, balanced force, instead of twelve million small ones.

Q: So what exactly is destiny?

AH: Destiny is the path set by your own spirit. It is the free will of your spirit. It only seems like something outside of free will to humans because the little human mind can't seem to find the controls, therefore deems the experience as something externally motivated.

Q: So it's not a destination?

AH: Destiny? A destination? Yes, perhaps, that is exactly what it is, just not compassed out with your human mind.

Q: But what is the goal?

AH: The goal is life and death, to experience...

Q: ...the ultimate paradox.

AH: No one has finished my sentences in a long time...
   You know with a silent, inner knowing what your destiny is. You are locked into a role, as I was, that is your own making.
   In answer to your question, why do the souls of all the holocaust participants have the right to haunt my soul?
   It was a part of the destiny for balancing the energy. They have earned the right to experiment with the manifestation of creation. They are being tested in spirit to be the ultimate peacemakers. I will hold a place here until all the millions have forgiven me. That will continue

to forge their union into integration and they will be a powerful peacemaking force to be reckoned with.

Q: Why did you choose us to talk to?

AH: You are a carrier of a message. Barbara has been specially trained to look this void in the face and uncover the mythology of evil. That is what the world needs. But you are staining yourselves in the eyes of culture by even thinking about associating with me.

When I was a baby, I had a small cut on my arm. I remember that cut. I was ordinary once in my life until I left behind my spirit to pursue my destiny in a human place, to fulfill my karmic responsibility.

It was all part of the plan.

Q: Can you tell us a little about the time that you lived with Eva Braun?

AH: Ah, this was a time of affluence, of trends about glamour and power, of turbulent, sweeping change across the face of Europe. The atmosphere that existed in the Third Reich was one that attracted odd elements of society–those who felt outcast–and gave them that external motivation for their feelings of depravity. Not unlike Mr. Versace and his clan, one of the powerful social classes at the time in Germany was the gays.

There were many openly gay men back then. My own sexuality was so far away from my conscious thinking: I did not consider myself to be any sexual preference. Yes, I had been with men, but I did not consider myself gay, for I was stirred to my depths by my beautiful Eva.

Eva was a part of my life that only spurred me to be darker. I was in such denial about what was happening, when Eva would step in, she touched me deeply and stirred me physically. She provided an oblique connection to the last remembered love I had felt, from my mother. I hated that, it made me aware of the absence within, the stark, insane vacuum.

Though I ached to have that part, that capability within me to feel, I did not love Eva. I needed her human touch to keep going. I was incredibly cruel to her in many ways and yet, in the end, it was she who hurt me. She was not true to me. She had other love interests, both men and women, which made me insane. Yet, when she was there, I lusted for her so, even through the pain.

Q: In light of what you're going through now, why did this happen to you, why did you ask for it to happen to you?

AH: Humans need to know what they are capable of creating. It is about perhaps one of the greatest challenges the human race must face: forgiveness. This is what will bring the balance.

Do you think the world understands? Do you think the world sees that they create these things? It was a group effort, the holocaust. I could not have done it alone.

Q: Yes, we know. And we're hoping to show them.

AH: Yes, you are, aren't you? And what of Hitler? Do you suppose anyone will forgive Hitler?

Q: But you said every one who was a part of the holocaust agreed to participate in this. I don't understand how it could then be your fault.

AH: Yes, but, it was still my fault, like it was Albert's "fault" that relativity came through his life, and Sigmund's "fault" that he brought sexuality to the forefront. Except they had nothing to "forgive" as I have.

Q: My husband doesn't believe that I'm talking to you right now.

AH: What could Hitler possibly say that would make him believe? You should be thankful he does not believe because it means he is not going to be dragged somewhere against his will.

No one will listen, and well, they shouldn't. They should listen only to themselves.

Q: Yes, they should but your words are going to shake them out of their cultural beliefs.

AH: Yes, one way or another. It may not be the actual words that I speak that will shake them. It may only be the idea of Hitler that some will listen to. I knew this before I agreed to speak, but then I knew many things before I came to life on earth.

Q: Can you give us some direction on answers to the question, "Why channel Hitler?"

AH: It is a good question. I am glad you ask it. Because from my unadulterated hell, I can remind you to never create this ever again. I can implore you from my place of eternal agony to never again allow yourselves to become as the world did when I was alive. Do you realize how many people looked past their own hearts to perform the acts? This was not just about Adolph Hitler pulling the triggers of seven million guns. This was about a culture following along blindly to what was dictated from a hidden place. Good men were drawn into the darkness, into their own hell, with varying levels of hell for each and every person who participated in this.

Talk to me so I can tell those today who are taking up the Nazi banners and marching in the street for hate and division, in the end, there will be only you, you and your hate and this burning fire. In the end, you will have to live with the repercussions of all the hate you generate for those around you, because ultimately, it is self-hate that you are persecuting others for, and that will return as your own karma.

You must learn how to never allow this to happen again. Only you can make sure, from a place of consciousness about your life now, that you make your choices with these things in mind.

This interview is also about forgiveness. If I represent the potential evil in all humans, then somewhere, inside each person is the capacity to perform such evil acts. You must forgive yourself this potential, first and foremost, for then you can forgive people such as me.

Q: You are a metaphor.

AH: Yes, I am a paradox and life is metaphor. I hold an anchor, believe it or not. To all I say, remember hell in your minds. To all I say, never forget me as a possible you.

Q: Thank you for your help.

AH: Don't go too far out on a limb for me. Ultimately, this is not about please and thank you. This is about a destiny.

You must thank all of those who braved coming into humanity at that time.

But you are welcome. And to you, I'd like to say good luck. For some reason, I think you will need it.

Ryan Wayne WHITE

December 6, 1971 - April 8, 1990

Gratitude, AIDS & Physical Healing

Q: Thank you, Ryan for talking to us.

RW: Hey, this is really a great honor! I never thought I'd be able to talk like this to people after I died. I mean, I thought a lot about death, and I knew God was going to take care of me, but, well, I have to say, it's pretty different than I imagined.

Q: What's so different about being dead than you imagined? And what did you think it was going to be like?

RW: I guess I thought that everyone was just kind of there, just hanging around. I see now that it really isn't much different than life. People here are pulled together with other people, for bigger reasons, to continue learning. No one just sits around, unless it's part of a rest plan. All of the activities in Afterlife are about creation, and manifesting creative energy. I guess I knew that when I was alive, but I never dreamt it would be so exciting.

Can you imagine what it feels like to sit at the table with *Albert Einstein?* Wow, that's some kind of dream come true for me. I really liked math, and I loved mechanical things. I still don't really understand why I am sitting here with these amazing people.

Q: Ryan, many of us think you were an amazing person yourself.

RW: I don't think I was any more amazing than anyone else who died of AIDS really. But I did get to be in the spotlight and carry a message about AIDS and gratitude forward, being that I got AIDS from a blood transfusion. People still judged me, as if I had done something immoral or something. I totally understood what gay people go through, even those without AIDS.

I think it was because I was so ordinary that it scared people to think a normal kid like me could get AIDS. It meant they could get it, too.

Q: Let's talk about your experience with having AIDS. Do you think you got AIDS for a reason, or was it just a random act of nature?

RW: Now, I totally believe I got AIDS as a gift. No, not the suffering part, and not the discrimination part. But the part where I got to carry this great message all over. I met so many people I never would have met. I got to talk to the world about things that other people wouldn't have heard. Let's face it, gay people have been speaking, yelling, suffering through AIDS for a long time without having people listen to what they are going through. So here comes this kid, a "victim" to this disease, talking about being grateful and making people listen.

But, would I have wanted to be normal when I was living? Oh, yeah. I often said I would trade my fame for just being an average kid, and getting to live an average life. I think maybe that's one reason I got to join in this party. It was like God was gifting me with a little reward in Afterlife for taking this message forward.

Q: As a child with AIDS, what did you think? Did you think you were being punished for something? And how did you feel as your friends and neighbors abandoned you?

RW: I tell you, what I went through was like hell. No one wanted to even touch me, well, except my mom and my real friends, my family who understood. When we first found out I had AIDS, the whole family was just floored. I was so young, and I guess I kind of understood at the time, but it wasn't until they didn't let me in school that it really started to hurt.

It's funny because I had AIDS for a long time before it started to really show. I had always been a skinny kid, it's not like I became some kind of ghoul, but the pain from the discrimination was almost worse than really getting sick. Guys who I played with from kindergarten said really hurtful things to me. Moms and dads actually rallied and worked to keep me away from their kids. It didn't seem to matter how much educational information we gave them, they just kept letting their fears lead them.

I was really gifted with this insight. Even as a thirteen-year-old kid, I could see the fear in their eyes. Since I knew I couldn't really hurt them, I felt bad for them, that they would think and act this way.

But that didn't stop me from crying. Thank God for my mom. She made me understand how special I was, and she always knew the right things to say that would help me sleep again, or help me stop crying. I know it was really hard on her, and I hated that, too, that she had to take the flak for what has happening to me. It became so absurd, you know? Like a mass hysteria, all surrounding me.

Q: When you moved away from Kokomo and resettled, did your life change?

RW: Yes, by then we were getting much more support from the media, and famous people were starting to get into the act. After we moved, there was not just an acceptance of us, but they actually welcomed us, as if we brought them some kind of notoriety.

Life did become easier, and still you would be surprised at how much this hatred of AIDS and homosexuality is a part of everyday life. Jokes, cartoons, comments in the grocery store, everywhere. When you're not infected with it, you don't notice as much.

My friend Judith used to talk to me about how special I was, that I had been chosen to carry this message to the world. She talked about courage a lot. She said I inspired her to love her own life more. All I knew was how much I really liked her, and suddenly she was my friend.

The same was true of Elton. He was such a great guy, he really loved me. We used to talk about being children, and about how he felt about being famous. He helped me a lot when the press got to be overpowering. I wanted him to be happy.

Q: Is there anything you want to tell him?

RW: Yes! Hi, Elton! It's really great here, just like you said! Remember those last conversations we had? I know I tried to tell you how much I loved you then, but I don't know if I ever really got to let you know how much your friendship meant to me.

It's just like we talked about, Elton, only way cooler. And I can still see you and hear you. It really is me you are talking to in the dark!

Elton is someone who gave me so much in the last days of my life. He was a complete softy, a real loving guy. He had lost so many friends to AIDS, and it was hard to see him go through this again. But I know how grateful he was to know me. And I sure was happy to have him for a friend.

Q: Tell us about courage. How did you find the courage to deal with all this?

RW: Courage isn't something you find, I don't think. I think it finds you. Sometimes, when your back is up against the wall, you really have no choice but to tough it out, to deal with whatever's in front of you the best way you can. That's all it felt like I was doing. I didn't really see myself as any great courageous hero.

My mom was the one who inspired courage in me. I could see what my illness was doing to her, and it made me really sad to think I was bringing this on her, and the rest of my family. I think she was the one with courage. On days when I would come home from school crying because they had been mean to me, she would be the one to rally. She was the one who taught me that I had to just be myself, no matter what I was, with courage and strength. I had to hold my head up and go on with another day, no matter what anyone said. I think I derived most of my courage from her.

Q: Ryan, even in all the turmoil and pain of your life, you maintained this attitude of being grateful. How did you do that, through all the pain of being ostracized and then through the ravaging of AIDS?

RW: When you're faced with something like AIDS, you get this perspective that normal, everyday life doesn't give you. You start to think that maybe this really is going to be your last day on Earth. So you live in the moment better: you don't want to lose one moment of life, knowing it could be your last.

Every day I would thank God for having that new day. And believe me, every new day was a miracle, after awhile, especially when I was the sickest. I made a point to ask God for one more day before I went to sleep. Each morning, I was so grateful that God answered my prayer with another day. Well, how could I not be grateful?

It's easy to forget sometimes that you are watched over. Even if you don't believe in God, hopefully there is at least one other person in your life that loves you. Lots of people take that for granted. I think human beings have a tendency to be self-centered, naturally concerned about their own well-being. That's different than being in charge of their own self-love. Self-centered people take the energy around them and suck it in. Self-loving people take the energy within them and put it out to the world.

My family and I knew we were here to bring this message to as many people as we could. We knew that everyone we touched, every last person in the grocery store or the gas station would be affected by what had happened to us. We felt called to help bring this message to as many people as we could.

I was really grateful for my family. I still am. I'm with my Mom a lot, and the cool part is, she knows it! She still talks to me! We talked a lot before I died, and I promised her I would be there, even after my body was gone. I guess we just didn't know how well we would be able to communicate! Hi Mom! I love you!

Q: What do you think AIDS is about? And do you think we will ever come up with a cure?

RW: I think that AIDS has already been cured. I guess that might sound cynical, huh? But I do. Having gone through what I did, I learned so much about how the government deals with this national, international really, health crisis.

I think there are so many more politics around finding a cure than anyone in the general populace knows. Ask anyone who has AIDS, especially homosexuals. They have been stonewalled, railroaded and bankrupted, completely overlooked in light of what really, honestly can be happening right now. Even when researchers do find information and new drugs about AIDS, they still make it almost impossible for the average person to have access to those drugs and treatments. That's because of the politics, and I'm really not sure what the answer is to that. You can't really bring down capitalism, but maybe with some more socially-aware people elected into office, you could make some inroads to uncovering the fraud behind the research.

As far as what AIDS is about, you have to be careful how you frame the answer to that. On one hand, it's a disease of a culture. I mean, there are only a few ways to really get AIDS. The number of accidents like I had are relatively small, compared to those who contract it through unprotected sex or sharing needles. Of course, since "innocent" people began contracting it through the blood supply, the fear level rose enough in "normal" people so that something started to get done about it. Before that, it was a slow course to bring about AIDS awareness to the public, because it meant bringing awareness of people others judged as deviants.

More energetically, I think it's a reflection of a dying part of society. There's energy in our culture that's very suicidal. Everyone predicts doom and gloom, and everywhere it seems like violence is up and people are killing each other. Even in spite of all the great stuff that happened at the end of the 80s with the opening of the world to freedom and independence, there's also been a dying in the culture.

Families began to isolate from each other, people became less like a community. What happened in Kokomo was a perfect example. People lived through their fears. I think AIDS is a reflection of that cry for help, for healing within our world on many levels.

Q: Do you think if we healed those things in our society, like homophobia and children killing children, that we could also heal AIDS?

RW: Yeah, I do, actually. I know it's a stretch, but think about all the facets of society that would change on top of each other. Like, if we could really inspire people to accept each other, and not delineate between sexual preference, skin color, or economics, we would all have a better chance of being happy ourselves, as individuals. Because no longer would you have to be subjected to someone else externalizing their fears onto you, and vice versa. You would be taking care of your own fears, not pushing them outside yourself, feeling even more victimized.

Without the discrimination, you have more people willing to work towards demanding the cure, wanting to put more money into making those drugs available to the sick. Mr. Sadat talks about changing society's focus from war to peace. Maybe all those military bases could be used as research facilities, or healing centers. I guess they might even be hospices. Let's put our energy and our focus into things that help to heal, and not tear down.

Q: Do you think there is purpose in physical illness? Or do you believe, as Christopher Reeve does, that it's all random, but what's important is what you make of it?

RW: I don't think it's random. I do think I got AIDS for a real good reason. The world changed a little because of what I did. I was just an ordinary kid, minding my own business in a Midwestern town, Sure, I was a hemophiliac and that kind of prepared me for some of the things about having AIDS, but for the most part, I was an average Joe. I can see how you might think it's random. The universe is pretty chaotic by nature.

But from where I am now? No, I don't think it was an accident. I believe I accepted the destiny before I was born as Ryan. I knew, on some deeper level, I was going to have to deal with this.

Q: Then why would you do that? Why would you agree to go into life knowing you were only going to get sick and die?

RW: Partly because, before being born, everyone is spirit. Everyone knows they are going to live through it. It's not like being human, where you don't understand yet what ultimately happens when you put your body aside. It doesn't sound nearly as dire in spirit. It's a life to live, to create, and to somehow try to influence the world, even if only in some small way. And the end result is that we're all going to die sometime.

On the other hand, while I knew I'd been asked to carry a message with me into life, I had little idea what it was going to feel like as a human being. That's why spirit comes to life, and why we create ourselves as humans, to feel all the suffering and joys of creation. When I was asked to carry this message, and if I wanted to be an inspiration in this way, I was excited! It was a chance to make a difference.

As soon as I was born, I lost all memory of making this agreement. When I got sick, and things started to happen, yeah, I used to ask, "Why me?" I thought sometimes it was just chaos, and I was the poor guy standing in the road when the truck came by and hit me. But I don't see things that way now.

Q: Do you believe that the physical body is basically a self-healing mechanism?

RW: Yeah, I do, and I think people are going to come on some real important discoveries in the new millennium.

The body is really a part of your expression of spirit. People don't know all the things their bodies can do because most people don't naturally like having a body. It takes too much upkeep, and there are always new reports of all the different things that can go wrong. That makes people afraid of what their body will do to them.

Being sick like I was gave me a new appreciation for my body. It was like a barometer for me. Because I was so sensitive, I sometimes felt like my body told me things. Like if someone was lying, or being two-faced, I always knew because my skin would feel tingly and I would get this tightness in my stomach.

Part of my own treatment for my sickness was to imagine. I used to daydream, especially when I was in the hospital and so weak. I really couldn't do anything but lie there. I used to do imagining, into my body, kind of like that movie, "Inner Space." I saw what all the AIDS molecules looked like, and I staged mock dog fights with the healthy cells. I really tried to see myself getting well.

When I took those guided tours into my body, I figured out a lot about other things as well. I imagined traveling into my own DNA and finding little circuit boards and switches, like I'd stumbled upon the control room. I would look for the switch that would start my immune system up, and then imagine feeling some big boiler somewhere fire up and be wiping out all those AIDS molecules.

But still, I died. But I don't think that's because the body isn't self-healing. I think it's just I needed to be who I was and have happen to me what happened for bigger reasons.

I know that science and medicine are going to discover some of the hidden secrets the body holds. All this work with regeneration is coming to the forefront. And the people here in spirit are working, too, on ways to bring all that information onto the Earth.

Q: Are there ways for humanity to help with healing? Or is it just hit and miss, some people will heal and others, like you, will be taken?

RW: You can't take my death as a sign of anything, really, except if you are looking at it from society's view point and not from this place of spirit. We as a human race keep bringing life to Earth so we can learn to make the physical world a true reflection of our spiritual world. To do that, we as humans have to learn to readjust our focus. It's that thing about fear: all my friends and the people in Kokomo who were so scared projected all their inner thoughts and feelings onto me. They didn't even know what they were doing, much less know how to stop and own their fear. My family and I never thought badly of them. I knew what it was like to be afraid, for sure. Mom always encouraged me to forgive them and be grateful for who I was and that I wasn't putting my fear back out on them. But that is your first reaction to fear, to strike back.

If everyone would look at themselves more closely, and see that their feelings about other people and the world are really about themselves, we would all heal ourselves more. Those people in Kokomo were just scared about getting AIDS themselves. But if they looked at it that way and learned to face their feelings and own them, they would have felt like they had more control, which was what they wanted in the first place. But instead, they exercised their control by trying to keep me away. In the end, they could keep me away all they wanted, but they were still afraid.

So the answers seem to lie in educating people, not just about the truth of AIDS, but about how they are hurting themselves by not taking full responsibility for how they feel, and seeing that it's ultimately only a reflection of their own relationship to themselves.

Jesus said, "Love your neighbor as yourself." I don't know how you can really love your neighbor if you have so much fear about just being alive.

I think God has a plan for everyone. I don't really think some people are covered in the plan and others aren't. My death had a big influence on many people. And now, since I'm not really dead, I can go on with the work I started on Earth.

Q: So you don't think people get sick as a punishment, or a karmic return of some kind?

RW: No, I don't. I know it's hard for you to understand, but being who I was was a really great honor. Yeah, it was tough, especially on my mom and my family, and the physical illness part was really hard, dying that way. But looking from where I am now at the big picture of my life, I know that I was blessed with a purpose in life and I know I rose to the occasion.

What everyone else took for granted I really had to work for. It was lots of work, just to live anywhere near a normal live. But it was the only life I had, so I just did the best that I could.

Norma Jean BAKER

June 1, 1926 - April 4, 1962

Feminism, Sexuality & Abortion

Q: Thank you for talking to us Ms. Baker.

NJB: Please, call me Norma.

Q: Norma, you rose to a place of influence in pop culture at a time when women's rights and issues were just beginning to move to the forefront. What role, if any, do you feel you might have played in bringing those issues into the conscious minds of America?

NJB: My place in American history served different purposes, really. For one thing, I was the epitome of popular, public sexuality. I'm not talking about sex, mind you, I'm talking about the sexual image women had at the time. I was like a go-between, from the time after World War II, when women had to return the power they got when the men were away at war, and the sixties, which, as we all know, was when women really began to stand up and speak their minds, and not be afraid of being openly, naturally sexual beings.

Not many people, I suppose, would look at me as some kind of icon of feminism. I can understand that. In many ways, I was the classic co-dependent, helpless female. That's certainly what most people got from my public image. Not many people knew the real, true me. My friends were often stifled from seeing me depressed. I didn't let many people know my mind. I ended up getting lost in my own public image, too, by the end.

Being famous is always a double challenge in dealing with life. There is the challenge of the public eye, always being looked at and commented on and photographed, and then the challenge to not let that feedback influence you to become what you perceive the world sees of you. That's what happened to me: I got lost to myself. I lost my intellectual power, as I became this public kitten.

The pain and sense of loss I sustained in my childhood set me up for the longing I felt through my entire life. I longed for something, all the time. I think you can see it in my eyes in some of those earlier pictures. That longing became the basis of a sexual positioning by people who were guiding me. But it was really an emotional longing more than a sexual craving. The emptiness I felt as a kid followed me around into adulthood because no one ever taught me any other way to fulfill myself than seeking outside myself.

As I rose from obscurity and into the public eye, the people around me started pulling my sexuality out of me. They wanted it to be a powerful part of displaying and selling me. They wanted me to exaggerate this natural side of myself so that I would appeal to more people.

I often thought back, later in life, to what I would have done, and what I would have been like had I not been brought up that way. What if I hadn't hooked up with those people who influenced me throughout my life? What if I had just been plain old Norma Jean? What if I had learned how to fill myself from my own self-worth and stayed home, married some strong, stable guy, had a bunch of kids and grew old and died in an old folks home somewhere, in my sleep. I can't tell you how many times I fantasized about that. Not that I wanted to give up any of what I had. It was a wild ride, I'm telling you. I wouldn't have given up any of it, but, you know, you often think about lives you could never live, just like I suppose many "ordinary" women fantasized about being me. What if I had been that ordinary woman? I don't know...

Looking back, I see now that I had a huge effect on the culture of sexuality in America. I did sort of make sexuality an everyday thing. Oh, I know the glamour was constructed, but I did have this very natural sexuality. I was comfortable in it. It did fill me; it was probably the one thing I knew was mine, that no one could take from me, that gave me a certain kind of power. Out of this need to feel something real like that in my life came my agreement to market it. The more successful I got through marketing this sexual part of me, the more I felt filled and powerful, and the more I wanted because, ultimately, it didn't fill me up. It was all empty calories and a very destructive cycle.

But I did gain power over many situations because of my sexuality. And don't think I didn't know it. I worked it to the hilt, in quite a creative way, I think. I took the softness of a woman, the completely feminine approach, the passivity, the compassion combined with the sexual appeal, and openly influenced things: everything from casual conversations to business deals. I could always gain the attention of a room, just by being Marilyn.

Not that I always got my way, but I did at least feel like I was a part of a world that basically ignored the rights of women. Using my power in this way hid my brain from their view. People usually didn't know how smart I was because I didn't want them to.

The only trouble was, this kind of power didn't work with my emotions, which were turbulent and extreme. I was a very unhappy woman, but I had to contain all that when I was in the public eye. For all the containment I did in public in order to portray Marilyn Monroe, I suffered terribly in private when I let my feelings out. That's why I used the drugs and the alcohol, because the price that I was paying for that power was isolating me from myself, from my true self.

But if you're just asking culturally, yes, I believe I set the stage for a much more open attitude about sex for women. My presence inspired women to know that their sexuality was not about performance, it was about being. A gal can be sexual anywhere, anytime. Not only that, but if a woman harnesses her sexual energy, great achievements can be created.

Q: What exactly do you mean by "harnessing sexual energy?"

NJB: First of all, girls were taught from the time they were born that they were suppose to get married. That was expected of a young woman during this era. For a long time, especially when I was in vogue, there was even an age we were suppose to be married by. Anytime past that age and a girl was an old maid. Even for those women who couldn't stay married to one guy, like me, there was a push to always have a man in your life.

What this does to a woman is focuses her fulfillment outside herself. It also encourages her to have sex when maybe she doesn't want to, or not have it when she does, and arranges her sexual identity around the guy. The focus of her own sexuality is now outside herself. She then becomes a product of that environment. If her guy likes lingerie, she buys herself some crotchless panties, whether or not they are a turn-on for her. She starts to mold her sexual identity around this thing outside herself, which is really foreign to her. Not just because she's trying to please this guy, but because she is taking on his image of what he thinks she should be. But he's a guy! He can only know what he wants her to be to him. He has no idea what she needs to be to herself.

So here she is, expending all this energy on becoming someone that she isn't, not getting what she needs from the guy, wondering why she is so empty even though she gives and gives and gives. That's when women turn to the booze and drugs, trying to not feel that emptiness anymore.

Q: Is this what happened to you?

NJB: Ah, yes, it was.

Q: Did you commit suicide or were you murdered?

NJB: Both. I was headed on a road of self-destruction almost from the time I was old enough to walk. There was so much sadness in my childhood, so much emptiness that had to be covered up and never talked about. I'm sure that's why I dreamt of being famous, to get me out of that place, to get me the acceptance and attention that I longed for as a kid.

Not that it was all bad, but I was a very introspective child. Like I said, in wondering what I would have been like had I been a normal kid, I thought, what happens to kids who feel this way? What do normal parents do for their children when they feel this vacant? I guess I thought there was some kind of perfect mom somewhere that could make everything make sense.

As a teenager, I learned what my sexuality could do. School was not a bad place for me, at least I was able to get attention. I found a place of acceptance on stage in the high school theater productions I was in.

When I started to really get notoriety, the longing only deepened, and that's when I began a slow spiral of medication and dulling the pain of the emptiness through gaining power from my sexual presence. I suppose there was a part of me that felt like a traitor, as if this insistence to put sexuality at the forefront of my image was hurting me in some way.

Did it really hurt me? I really don't think it would have had I been more emotionally stable. If I'd had a real sense of self-worth, I don't think the sex part of my persona would have felt so betraying. But I was caught in the projection that if the world saw me as sexy and beautiful, and I could have power over them by being what they wanted me to be, then I must really be all those things. But let me tell you, you can have the whole world hailing you as a goddess and if *you* don't believe it, well, it just doesn't matter. It has no effect upon you.

I ended up wanting more and more. I became insatiable. To quiet the longing, at first I drank. Then came the kind of power that I probably didn't need: people attending to my every wish. They got me a doctor, at first to help with the insomnia. From there grew a dependency on him which lasted until my last breath.

Did I commit suicide? Did he murder me? Like I said, both. On one hand, my doctor just didn't understand what else to do, considering the accepted means of dealing with this kind of woman. Remember, this was a time when women were sentenced to mental hospitals for being too emotional. The last thing I wanted was that. And yet, you see where my life took me.

I truly didn't understand the kind of tolerance I had built up in my body. The more drugs I took, the more I wanted and needed, until, at the end, I overdid everything. My entire system was saturated through the years and years of using.

On the other hand, as far as murder went, my doctor was being influenced by outside sources. I was very suspicious, of everything, in the last years of my life. I knew that because of my involvement with the Kennedys that the government had a closer eye on me than most. Can you imagine someone like me being so close to the President and a well-known U.S. senator, who happens to be his brother, in this day and age? The kind of scrutiny on me was appalling but understandable. I mean, I was very close to the President and could have been a great security risk.

Then there were the others, the ones who eventually killed Jack, who were also trailing me. It didn't make it any easier that these men who followed me and spied on me were getting off on the fact that they were assigned to Marilyn Monroe. It was really a sick feeling for me. But, of course, because of my unstable state, everyone imagined I was paranoid, even schizophrenic.

So, yes, my doctor came to my house and spent six hours with me. He essentially murdered me by pushing along what seemed like a natural course of actions that I would have taken. For me to eventually die of a drug overdose would not be questioned, considering my history of being "unstable."

The same people who took out Jack influenced my doctor early on. They had a bigger sway in the whole big scheme of things than anyone knew. They blackmailed him, telling him they had connections that could incriminate him in several other cases he had and the way in which he was administering drugs.

Q: So you're saying that the same people that assassinated President Kennedy somehow paid off your doctor to give you a little too large a dose of barbiturates?

NJB: It was a combination of several drugs, but yes, that's what I am saying. I was too great a risk to them and their plans. It was easy for them, though, I made it very easy for them. And truly? If they hadn't, I probably would have ended up overdosing anyway.

Q: It was rumored that you had several abortions. Is that true, and how did you feel about abortion?

NJB: Yes, I did have several abortions. I don't think it was any big secret, although we tried to keep it out of the press.

I was so far away from my real feelings, I found it easy to use abortion as a form of birth control. Since I was so disconnected from my feelings, I would not deal with the emotional side of abortion. I only allowed myself to look at my career and my power, and the fact that, in a daydream, yes, I wanted kids. As that normal Norma Jean I might have really loved being a mom. But in the life I was in, the idea of having to focus my attention on raising a child was not very appealing to me. And yet, you can see, from the emptiness inside, the *idea* of a child served to fill me, just like the attention and the fame served me.

But the difference between the two lives was too great. I could not see how I could merge a family life with the life I was living as Marilyn Monroe. What would happen to my sexual image if the world saw me pregnant? Back then, one did not fit with the other. I was risking losing my entire life if I had children.

Those were very hard decisions, and yet, each time I became pregnant I found out what I really wanted. In my position, it wasn't difficult to have my doctor perform the surgery. It was hell on my body though. I took long periods to recover from them, and of course, my emotions roller-coastered and I fell deeper into drink and drugs.

I didn't really struggle with the moral issues. I didn't ask myself, "Am I taking a life? Am I committing murder?" I struggled more with the loss of the emotional piece of me that was the mom. My body rebelled, and my heart was very sad, but I didn't think a lot about if I was going to hell for it. I felt like I was in hell anyway, so it didn't matter.

Nowadays, abortion seems to be something much more powerful than it really is. People take it as an issue and use it to create division. More times than not the doctors and nurses giving the abortions become targeted as killers. What about the women who are pregnant? What happens to them? This misplaced blame in society comes from a lack of respect for the women.

I'm certainly not saying those women should be targeted as the killers. I'm saying that hard core abortion opponents don't respect the power and the rights of the women as the overseers of their own bodies. So how can they expect us to believe they respect the life they claim they are trying to save when they don't respect the woman who carried that fetus, or the doctor at the clinic?

I can guarantee you, every single woman who faces the possibility of abortion looks into the mind of God. She *is* the creator, for all intent and purposes. She is the one with the morning sickness and the labor pains, she is the one with the bills, she is the one who has to take care of that new life when her husband leaves her for a younger woman. It's the woman who is ultimately left in charge, only culture does not credit her as such. This is the change that needs to take place now, not wrestling over whether it's moral to have an abortion.

Q: From where you are now, is there a moral justice around abortion? Is it considered murder in that place of spirit to take the life of the fetus?

NJB: If you really want me to answer that question, you had better be prepared to have people misunderstand this.

Q: Oh, I think we are prepared to have many people misunderstand many things the Party of Twelve says.

NJB: Okay, well, just so I warned you.

The soul that I am, Norma Jean, came and went in life on Earth, with the body I had, the life, the pain, the whole agenda that I brought with me as that tiny little baby. I didn't know, in my thinking, that I had this agenda, but I did bring it with me.

To begin with, my soul did not enter my body permanently until I took my first breath. Before that, I was a part of the creation of my fetus. My spirit was working with many things, many forces—science, physics, magic, intention, and the souls of my parents—

to create this fetus in the womb of my mother. She and I, on spirit level, were working together. If you have ever been pregnant, you know, you can feel the spirit of the child hovering around when you're pregnant. In the time in the womb, the soul of that child does hover, going in and out of the newly-forming body, sort of like a hummingbird building a nest.

So it's a cooperative thing, the mother and the soul of the new child, science at work regenerating cells, and the divine intention of life to create itself anew. It's a great time to work in, to be in. It's too bad we forget about this process. I guess, since we have no conscious minds to retain the information, we don't often recall it, even as early childhood memories. Although I sometimes used to think I could remember what it was like being in the womb.

Sometimes, for whatever reason, abortion, miscarriage, illness, whatever, the growing fetus doesn't reach the point where it can sustain human life. Then the soul of the new child undergoes a refocusing time. But all the work and energy and cooperation spent building the fetus was not lost or in vain. The soul, being eternal by nature, starts to arrange a difference entrance onto the planet, sometimes with the mother at a later date, sometimes with different parents.

For me, I believe that soul that was building a life in me was the same one all the time. There was no sadness on her part for not coming into physical form through me. I suppose that's because we both learned what we needed to learn. She helped me a great deal to touch compassion in my life, and I helped her learn about the manifestation of physical form. She did eventually come into life with someone else.

The Universe can be cruel through the eyes of humans. But from a place of spirit, human life becomes cruel when someone does not strive to love. That seems to be the bottom line for being human. Since I couldn't find respect in my own image of myself, I had to trust the people around me. They all told me to have the abortions. That part remains very sad to me, even now.

Q: Why do some people have miscarriages and some don't? And what happens to those miscarried souls? Are they any different than the soul of abortions?

NJB: No, they're the same. Yes, in the case of a miscarriage, there's a different way the fetus is aborted through what you might consider to be circumstances "beyond your control." From a place of spirit, both your soul and the soul of the new child are in agreement about this. But try and tell that to the conscious mind of a mother who just miscarried a longed-for fetus. The pain the event inflicts upon her conscious mind is just another way to challenge her to remember this infinite Universe.

Q: Let's go back to feminism for a moment. Do you think that there is any real hope for women getting recognition in this culture for being equal to men? Do you think the power structure is just too patriarchal for that to ever happen, or can we somehow make a difference, and bring a return to balance of culture in this area?

NJB: Well first off, women are not equal to men; we are more powerful. Now, before everyone loses their minds over this, let me explain.

In the social order of things, men have traditionally been the power holders. They have had the dominance over women that the stronger of the species should. They were stronger in physical form and more enduring, and when it came time to fight, it was their strength that preserved the tribes, the family.

But in this culture, there isn't much talk about the power of the feminine infrastructure. Women uphold the basic infrastructure of modern society. They not only still perform the duty that has been theirs through time that no man can take away, which is childbearing, but they now, too, are physically stronger than ever before. Women fight in armed conflicts, manage large corporations, perform heavy manual labor. Women have successfully infiltrated the fields that men have traditionally dominated.

But men will never be able to bear a child. It's that simple. And it's not about being good enough, or strong enough, but it's just all in the plumbing. It was part of God's plan that you can't argue with, not like you can debate whether a woman is strong enough to be in the military. There is no arguing the fact that men don't bear the children.

This doesn't make us better than men. I mean, face it, you need to have the man to make the child to bear. But it does put women in a position of more power, simply because of the capacity of their nature to bear life.

Men can now stay home and do the child nurturing, at least easier than they could when I was a woman. Imagine asking Joe to give up his career and stay home all day with the children! These changes are helping balance the power, too, but for the most part, women work the power from the inside out.

Q: Do you think using one's sexuality as a part of the whole package of who you are is demeaning, or empowering?

NJB: Well, that depends on the rest of the package. If you're walking into a place where you want to be invisible, where you want to blend into the woodwork, you wouldn't play up your beautiful breasts. On the other hand, if you want to distract people from knowing how onto them you are, you might want to highlight your breasts, knowing that it will draw people away from seeing you are this smart cookie, allowing you a little more leverage in how you can react.

Sexual image is about environment. Had I been around in Victorian times, I would have been ostracized as a whore for being so openly sexual as I was. In your modern culture, I'm hardly even a blip on the screen of sexual explicitness. So you can *think* you'll be using all your assets if you go to your corporate meeting with a business plan and a short skirt. But if you walk into that environment and short skirts are indicators of someone being less intelligent, they won't be able to see your brains, no matter how smart you talk.

But here we're talking about the calculated use of your sexuality, like I did. That isn't necessarily the best thing for every woman. And it certainly isn't the way to mold your own sexual energy because, here again, you're looking at the environment and adapting your energy flow to it, rather than reaching deep inside yourself and seeing who it is you truly are, and then just being that person. I suppose it all depends on what you're after in life.

Q: How can we as women in the new millennium mold ourselves into healthy sexual beings?

NJB: You can start by serving yourself. Do away with having sex for awhile and experience your sexuality without giving it away to anyone, without expending it anywhere. Sexual energy is very defining, very creative, very filling.

The challenge with this is that you'll have to feel all the emotions that surround it. See, that's one reason why people have sex, because it distracts them from feeling just the purity of their own energy and all the life around that energy. It's not that your emotions are keyed on your sexuality, but they all work in tandem: sexuality, emotions, intellect. They all work together. To deny your sexuality forces you to deny what you think and feel about your sexuality as well.

No one can take your sexual energy from you. Before you're born you buzz with what will become the major part of your sexual being. After you die, you bring that vibe into spirit with you. Like Sigmund says, it's an inner gravity that helps your spirit identify itself. When you come into life, you bring it with you, along with your sexual agenda.

Some people bring with them a strong feminine vibration. I did, maybe too strong! But when that feminine energy is born as a boy, a great conflict of interests is created with this society. Boys are culturally raised to identify with a certain set of sexual vibes. Out of fear of being called a "homo" and humiliated, little boys first close off their intellects, about that sexual energy, then their emotions become fearful, and eventually they fall into line and allow themselves to be molded around that cultural definition, or they go against it, and end up outcasts.

Women who come with strong masculine agendas don't seem to fare quite so poorly as feminine men. Culture right now is really confused about sexuality as a rule.

But this agenda is what makes someone gay or straight. It's dependent on the many items in someone's agenda for their life.

Whoever you are, if you really take some time out of your life and be with your own sexuality, get to know it, let it bring up the fears, then look at the fears, give your emotions time to embrace those fears and enlighten them, and have the courage to intellectually be your own person, you can create a much more healthy relationship to your sexuality than I had.

The great part about the new millennium is that it's so open. There's room now for lots of unusual things in the mainstream. These are exciting and stimulating times you're living in.

Q: Norma, I read somewhere that you and Shelly Winters shared an apartment when you were first starting out, and when she asked you who you wanted to go to bed with, you said Albert Einstein. Why was that?

NJB: Albert is, as I always imagined, a very stimulating man. I loved men with great minds. Arthur Miller was a fabulous companion. Joe and I touched more compassionate parts of each other. But Albert always seemed to me to be light-years ahead of everyone else, and so unafraid to be a revolutionary. From what I read about him, he was a lot like me in many ways, as far as the public expecting things from him. Only instead of sexuality, they wanted his intellect to be the attraction. Everyone always expected him to be smart, when he really would have liked to have been sexy. I was always thought of as so sexy, but I was honestly a very bright woman. Not many people knew that about me because they didn't want to see past the images.

So in a vague way I could relate to Albert. And he is, in spirit, as stimulating as a girl could imagine!

Oh, and he discovered the theory of relativity in the same year I was born. I always fancied that fact.

Q: Norma, is there anything you want to say to the women of today to help them experience a fuller sexuality or to be more comfortable with who they are sexually?

NJB: I would only say, spend some time with yourself. Especially when you feel out of balance, or if you feel lost to your own sexuality. Remember there are so many layers of your personality to work through. And remember that sexuality is different than sex. Sex is a control dance; sexuality is the inner feeling of being alive, of vibration, of sense of self, that no one can take away from you.

And remember that you're beautiful no matter how ordinary you are. I would have been a knockout as normal Norma Jean, too. But not because of my body, but because I would have been truly happy. And that's the most attractive thing you can be.

Sigmund FREUD

May 6, 1856 ~ September 23, 1939

Psychology, Dreams & Sexuality

Q: Thanks for speaking to us, Mr. Freud.

SF: Sigmund would be better, please.

Q: Sigmund, knowing what you know now, are you finding that your theories on dreams and such don't really apply?

SF: No, I don't find that at all! But I do look upon those times of discovery with great longing. Those were times of inception, it was not expected of me that I understood everything then. My purpose was to open doors, open doors. The difficulty came when it was time to process all the information and sketch the relationships of the parts of self to each other and one another.

Dreams are exactly what I discovered, only more. Bigger than I thought. Much bigger than I even thought back then.

Q: But I thought that the emphasis of your work on dreams was sexual. Now I'm learning that they are really messages and interpretations of life that don't have anything to do with sexuality.

SF: Oh, but that is where you are wrong! They have everything to do with sexuality, but very little to do with the cultural interpretations of that sexuality, the very interpretations I began.

The dreams are manifestation of the sexual energy of your physical body. In the dream state, it is your sexual energy that brings you back to you. Sexual energy is like having your own gravity.

What wasn't exactly correct was my interpretation of what sexual energy meant against the culture I was living in at the time and also with regard to my personality. I was extremely compulsive and exceptionally obsessive. Certainly I can credit my diligence and perseverance into an undiscovered area of reality to those traits. But it was that very compulsion that prevented me from realizing how much projection I was involved in. Much like Adolph's projection of his lack of emotions, I projected my personal neurosis over the theories I was developing.

Q: So you're saying that we define ourselves in our dream state by our sexuality. Is it about desire or is it an energy the individual exudes?

SF: Sexuality is the life force of the body. Humans are meant to exist in a vibration that feels like pure orgasm. That is part of what heaven is, but, well, how can anyone think to be in heaven when they cannot be with their own bodies and their own sexuality?

The finely-tuned vibrations of your sexual energy reveal a road map to a molecular level, a road map to the source of your own intelligence. Your sexual energy is the key to that road map.

But culture makes it about morals and meaning, rituals of union or not, having to pick it apart psychologically. Culture takes acts of sex and labels, judges, confines and forbids them, removing all the acceptance and mystery from something that is far more scientific than moral.

In my early work, I was beginning to investigate avenues to dissociate from culture. I knew that the inner life was symbiotic to the outer life. But I was not sure that we as humans had the integration and strength of character needed to envelop such personal power as to dissociate from culture. After all, look at the atrocities of the World Wars. There was nothing in my investigations that indicated society could properly use that kind of personal power justly.

Instead of investigating further, to see if we could cultivate the strength to take on changing culture, I took that embryonic idea, projected that everyone's inner life was as neurotic as mine and concluded that humans were elementally weak!

So, did I understand the metaphysical interpretations of sexual energy back then? Heavens no! And good thing! I wasn't supposed to!

Q: Why weren't you supposed to know it back then?

SF: Because it would have been inappropriate for where I was on my path at the time. I was too neurotic. By projecting my own neurosis, I was able to catalyze an entire generation of investigators into taking these ideas further. My own students began the evolution of my material, right under my nose.

I was always the grounded one, you know, the one who thought too much. In school, I was always last, finishing tests, in line for lunch, late for appointments. My mind became so myopic about whatever it was that I was engaged in, I took a long time to follow up with people. I often felt I actually moved slower or that I was behind the times, even in the face of all my degrees and credentials. But those degrees were ones I created for myself. I just followed a little niche that drew me in, and there I landed, in that place, at that time, making sweeping statements about my own neurosis.

Q: Can you tell me a little bit about what place psychotherapy has in our lives, as a society?

SF: Thank you, I was hoping to get a chance to expound upon some of the misconceptions that have been accepted from my previous work.

The culture I lived in was the stiff Victorian era of class breeding and social mores. People did not think for themselves. Society was plagued with divisions. When I began to turn inward and realize the multi-capable functions of the inner self, I felt like an anthropologist, mining into the richness of this secret inner life. Formulating the structure of the inner self, people started asking who they really were, and asking it from an intellectual point of view, within the classes of the culture.

Using drugs helped open me even further to access my inner riches. Understand, at that time, drug use was viewed with more leniency. Soda companies made bottled drinks that basically contained cocaine. It was not difficult to obtain the drugs I used. Ultimately, though, they were merely a tool for viewing the world from outside the box. This I found of great assistance to my work.

The birth of this focus inward was absolutely necessary to coming to where you are now, integrating that spiritual essence and that human mind, knowing self as you could not know without that knowledge of psychology.

Psychology is about to make a great evolutionary leap!

Q: Would you change anything about psychotherapy knowing what you know now?

SF: The idea, I believe, is for psychotherapy to evolve into what it truly was always meant to become: a road map inward to complete self-responsibility. When that happens, psychology will become obsolete. Psychology will then become the needless vaccine to eradicate illness when we have mastered self-healing.

Q: Can you talk more about the molecular level of sexual energy and vibration?

SF: Yes, I was hoping you would ask me to!

Unlike the ideas I generated in person, which had to do with the dramatization of sexuality, in spirit, I now see where I was missing the mark. The sexual energy is independent of environment. In fact, it creates the environment, instead of being created by an external influence.

Sexual vibration is unique in every single person, like a fingerprint. So, when you meet someone whose sexual energy is matching or closely associated with yours, and you come together, you are stirring the primordial soup and grinding your vibrations together, matching them in tone, creating the emotional needs and the visual desires. Then you literally explode together. The potential is life. The potential by-product of male and female stirring the sexual vibrations is the creation of life. That is like a sexual comet tail, the essence of being a human being.

Now, this double, partnered energy is different than the gravity of self.

Q: When you say "gravity," do you mean seriousness, or the laws of physics?

SF: From within your body originates your vibrational fingerprint. This vibration, which is specific to you, emanates outward, and from those waves come the formation of the matter that makes up your skin and your bones and all of the parts of your physical body. You simply cannot be, and not be sexual energy. This is what I mean by your inner gravity.

Q: Is the first step to molecular cell regeneration?

SF: Yes, I am proud to say it is! And that is why what I discovered when I was living still applies! The stages of human evolution that involve psychology are leading to a renewed journey into the physical body as well, into the very depths of the DNA. So you see, all of the rhetoric of my work on Earth served to open the doors to the eventual discovery of a deeper knowledge, past the conscious mind, past the act of sex and into the instincts of the body.

Being human is the key to unlock the mysteries of sexuality, compassion and divinity. All of these come through the human body. To change the supporting culture around you, embrace this journey of discovery.

Remove the bonds of judgment from your sexuality and dispel the myth of external validation.

You are also being challenged with the age of the computer.

Q: This is a challenge? How so?

SF: Yes, it is. It's a test to see if you can detect the different evolutionary phases occurring right under your noses! Look at the Internet, this place where the world comes together in a nanosecond. This is the reflection of the dreamtime maps.

Q: We love the Internet.

SF: Of course! We do too! We find it delightfully accommodating!

Much of my investigation into sexuality and its link to culture was spurred by my lucid dreaming. Dreamtime reveals the map to the DNA. My own dreams were highly sexual in nature, which triggered the neurosis, which effectively prevented me from going very far out of my body. I felt trapped, each time I went to dream, by the limits of the culture I lived in.

Part of my problem was that I was not like Albert. I felt much more uncomfortable not being accepted into culture. Perhaps that is why I obsessed about it so. I wasn't in denial about people thinking I was nutty. And yet, those of us who knew each other, and understood what we were doing, we were the anchors in the storm together. But I did not ever feel comfortable being on the cutting edge of culture. I felt instead a great deal of pressure to live up to the expectations of my position. It was a great deal of stress.

It went to my head, and I found myself being drawn into interpretation through ego, and unfortunately an entire basis of psychology was built solely around my phobias.

Q: So when Christopher Reeve has dreams about walking again, it's a sign that he actually will?

SF: Well not necessarily, but that kind of molecular regeneration, as a self-motivated function, begins in the dreams.

Your sexual fingerprint vibrates thought into matter. When you are dreaming, you are in the soft body, or the insulation body, but you still retain your fingerprint. From that dream state, as your sexual energy begins to formulate into matter, the reality of that dream slips into a firmer molding. The sexual energy surging through the dream lights the fires that create the ignition of manifestation of matter in its densest form: Human life!

So, yes, as Mr. Reeve has dreams of walking, he is vibrating thought into matter, and it is first showing up in his soft body. He walks in his dreams. Not only does he view himself walking, but he experiences that same reality of lucidity that I did in my dreams. He brings his fully-functioning spinal chord one step closer to form in his hard body, or his waking state.

In this way, you will all learn to dream your way to heaven!

Q: If each of us is involved in our own destiny and creating our lives, why is it that Hitler is held responsible for the Holocaust? I mean, if we each choose our lives, aren't we all responsible for our own participation?

SF: This is, believe it or not, the age old question! On one hand, this is evolution we are talking about. We are in the process of upgrading perhaps to a finer version of ourselves.

On the other hand, humanity abides within certain rules as well. For every action, there is an equal and opposite reaction. What Adolph did as a human had certain undeniable consequences. It is not that he is victim to the ones who dominate him. Those consequences were part of the agreement in terms of destiny.

He remains today a part of the continuing experiment of bringing balance to both spirit and humanity. He still challenges people to be compassionate and forgiving. As he said, until the souls of everyone he harmed have forgiven him, he will remain in his hell.

But I have heard that some people believe it's dangerous to think of Adolph as a child. Why would this be, except to prevent you from feeling compassion for him? And what if you were to feel compassion for him, as "evil" as he was? Would this mean you were being "evil" too?

What is the point of the human race holding in their hearts such contempt, for anyone? You then become the vessels of contempt. You then allow yourself to be filled with the very energy you are judging as evil!

The idea has always been to bring the conscious thinking into alignment with the divine being within. So, yes, in the long run, all of us, including Adolph, and the souls of the collective consciousness of the holocaust victims, we are all fine here in spirit, still working toward balance. But as co-creators of our own lives on Earth, we are still absolutely held responsible for everything we created for ourselves on earth. We did create chaos in our own ways, each and every one of us.

In learning to build a better mousetrap, what would you do if you found someone stuck in that mousetrap? Would you stand and without compassion tell him that he must have wanted to get in that mousetrap, and then sit back and watch him suffer? No, quite hopefully, in a civilized culture, you would stop and help him out of the trap, regardless of who created it. In that way, it is a test for you.

Ultimately, this is about merging the intentions of the human mind with the unconditional love of Spirit. We are all in the process of creating this.

Q: So we can heal ourselves before we make the mistakes?

SF: Yes yes, that is the idea! For those of us in spirit waiting to return again to the human race, we are offered the hope that we can do it better now. For those of you with bodies, you can keep aligning your human thinking to the voices of divinity.

Then, it's all in how you judge these "mistakes" we made ... me, and Adolph, and Albert, who, don't forget, brought the world the knowledge of mass destruction. It doesn't matter if it's the genius of Albert, or the evil of Adolph. We all made "mistakes." It is so important to learn from mistakes in order to make them useful.

Q: What can you tell us about the Party of Twelve?

SF: Specifically, we are an association of souls, assembled because of our dedication to ingenuity and evolution, to science and to possibility, brought together to work to unlock the codes within DNA. All of us here have chosen to work in this association to help bring you information about the true nature of human power.

Each of us brings to the Party a field of expertise, a part of the mold of being human, and the reciprocal paradoxical positions as well. So, for example, I bring to the table advanced knowledge of the sexual vibration, as well as the need to heal the planet of the misconceptions my first body of work imposed. We intend to skew the limited perception you have of your human life in order to help remove its cultural embrace. We want to change the way humans think about their power through the archetypal representation of all good and all evil that the twelve of us, as former humans, hold.

The Twelve might better be described by Buckminister Fuller. I was much more concerned about the symbols of dreams as a reflection of the mind and sexuality, and connections between dreams and the waking world than I was with numbers or geometry. Generally, the energy of the twelve in relationship to each other generates the power to create physical form. And look! Look at us in action! Writing a book together, from beyond the grave, no less!

By the way, we want to tell you that we are preparing a place here for Bucky. He will be with us soon. We are all very excited.

Q: Are there twelve of us on Earth as well?

SF: Yes, you will work with your own Party of Twelve in the living breathing flesh, not just us old dead fogies. You will be brought together with those who will serve as your support systems. In the meantime, seek out cooperative associations of people, and teach yourselves to work peacefully together.

Q: Why are you talking to us? I still stand in wonder, why us?

SF: Yes I know, I often asked that question. I often thought, I was not the humble one, nor was I the bright one. I was the stuffy fellow with the dirty mind and the obtuse view of how things ran together. I was aloof. I thought I was better than everyone else, all the while terribly insecure, as expressed through my compulsions.

When I was alive, society was so vapid, so surreal in many ways. Hitler and the war were a picture of hell, this is true. But the atmosphere around the continent leading up to those incidences was extremely exciting from a scientific vantage point. The early 20th century brought so many advances in medicine and research, in molecular understanding. That was truly what you might call the New Age.

But I was not sure always of where to stand, how to be. So I just wondered, why me? And believe me, here in spirit, being given the opportunity to speak again, I am still asking, why me?

Q: Thank you, Sigmund.

SF: It's been entirely my pleasure!

Anwar al-Sadat

December 25, 1918 ~ October 6, 1981

Disarmament & Peace-Making

Q: First of all, it's a great honor to be here with you today, Mr. Sadat.

AS: It is my pleasure. This era that you are in is truly exciting, so much different than the time when I was so diligently working for peace in the Middle East. To have this opportunity to speak again, from this new perspective, is indeed a special privilege.

Q: Mr. Sadat, you must have known back then, when you were working toward changing the culture of your world, that you were basically writing your own death sentence by standing up for peace like that. Why did you do it? What made you want to risk your life in that way?

AS: From a very young age, I felt called to this "special mission." Even growing up in the environment of Arab vs. Jew, I knew I was destined to make some kind of stand about unity, though it was difficult to talk about as a child.

A person such as yourself is sometimes told by some religious factions that, because you are using your talents and insights to talk to me posthumously that you are talking to demons or the devil. Imagine growing up in an atmosphere where you have to be careful of who you tell about your thoughts of peace and unity. It might mean being harmed or killed by a faction of society that can then slip into the fabric of their rhetoric, and evade the law.

I first remember the colonialism in the Middle East by Britain and France. I was greatly intrigued by the energy of Europe, since early in my youth. The Peace Conference in Paris in 1919 was a well-told story in my home. Then came World War II, with Germany invading North Africa. This brought together many rebel factions of Arabs, some that had previously been fighting one another.

For as long as I can remember, the Middle East has had a pervasive atmosphere of violence. Government was run in a somewhat terroristic way. I myself was guilty of working within that kind of cultural system. I was not completely free of falling prey to the influences of terrorism as an arm of law and order.

Having a government wrapped in its religion was both a blessing and a curse. So many in the Middle East could not imagine church and state being separated, and many felt that was the downfall of the West: so little contact between the religious factions and the political factions.

And still, it is those very alliances that birth holy wars.

Q: As a child you said you knew you were going to be a peacemaker. How did you know this?

AS: I was raised by two people who were, without a doubt, products of their culture. As I said, as a child, I heard much about this famous peace conference. So much of my fantasy centered around somehow bringing all the factions of war to the table, and reigning victorious as I systematically designed my make-believe peace. Ever since I was little, I wanted to understand both sides of the conflicts.

My self-image of peacemaker moved me along in adulthood. I was charismatic in a very earthy way. I felt frankly more comfortable with the peasants than with the government officials and religious men. I knew the ordinary people, the mothers and the fathers, needed to be seen as that: ordinary people, not as some faceless society run by a government making sweeping dictates. Keeping close to that idea, I eventually made my way to a position of power, where I was able to exert this peacemaking influence to create a peace that I so yearned to see come about.

A part of me was still caught in the "eye-for-an-eye" reasoning of the previous generations. Part of me believed I had to finally fight a war for Egypt with our arch enemy, Israel, and win. But even in military actions, I found it beneficial to understand the minds of my enemies.

After Nasser's loss in the Six-Day War, we were an outraged, yet weary nation. When I first took power and began a tour of the military bases, I talked to the soldiers, not as commander-in-chief, but as one brother to another. That is one enduring aspect of the Arab world: as many factions that have fought amongst us, there is a strong sense of brotherhood and nationalism in our blood. I looked into the eyes of my frontline soldiers, some with children and wives of their own. I could feel their pain, their worry about their families. Some of these soldiers were only boys themselves.

As I talked to them, I started to further develop the ideas of my childhood. In retrospect, I was tuning into the destiny that I had brought with me. Just like our friend Adolph, I knew I had come here to play the part of a man who would change culture. I have to admit I chose one of the most enduring and violent cultures on Earth. As I ruled this ancient, powerful, rich country, with her longtime battles with Israel, I started to wonder why we were fighting. Aside from the heritage of violence and a history of dissension between us, I began to wonder what was beneath the religious rhetoric and misplaced patriotism.

I partook of searching through archives and talking to the country's religious leaders. Of course, this had to be done secretly and in a very roundabout fashion. I wanted to know where the roots of the Arab-Israeli conflicts began. They stretch so back far through history, I found it impossible to pinpoint the incident that started the fighting in the first place. After all, the Israelis were once a tribe from Egypt. No matter how much history I poured over or how many conversations I had, I could not comfortably find the beginning.

Then, it hit me. It did not matter the root. Here it was, years and years and years of fighting, of Holy Wars, of death and destruction, killing sons and husbands in the name of what? Allah? In the name of simply being an Arab? Were we not human beings first, and then Arabs and Israelis, Americans and Soviets? This was traitorous language for the leader of one of the most powerful Arab nations in the world.

As I toured the military facilities and talked to the soldiers, and thought about what I believed in my heart, I knew I had to change something.

I believe it was at that time, in that early formulation of the plan, before the war in 1973, that I knew I would be assassinated. I knew there was absolutely no way that I could make this change and expect that, in this time period, everyone would understand or support it. It is not in the Arab nature to put down the weapon. There is a great interpretation of Islam that believes in martyrdom as an act of God. I knew I was not going to appeal to those parts of society, and I knew how they usually dealt with their enemies.

But what could I do? Here I was, standing in front of line after line of men of many ages, men with families. I couldn't understand the reasoning: I was sending them out to probably die at the hands of the enemy. I started to think that, by doing that, the enemy only won. It was the greatest loss of our most precious natural resource, these men, and I did not want to see any more Egyptian blood shed in the name of war.

Along with this was the reality that our natural resources were drying up, employment was low, and the very state of the state was not one that could continue to support the economics of war. I knew we needed to align ourselves with one of the super powers to prevent this war from going on into the future of yet another generation of Arabs and Israelis.

That is when I started to dare to see things in a different way. I began to formulate my peace plan much before it ever got to the table. The first step was to make a decision as to which super power to align Egypt. At this time, many of our neighbors had aligned with the Soviet Union. There was some sense to this, due to the close proximity of the continents, their natural resources, the alliances of our neighbors, the great might of Communism. I could reasonably consider this direction.

But I have to admit, there was so much personal freedom in the West that was appealing. Not just freedom to not have to live under a military state, but all of the inventions, the creativity, all of the arts, the ability to protest. I followed the Vietnam War closely. I watched how the United States dealt with their own dissidents. It was miraculous to me, in many ways, this freedom.

You, as a country, were appalled by what happened at Kent State. By that time, I was already partnering with the West, but I was amazed that these four people had such an impact. In the Arab countries, many people die every day in acts of terrorism by governments, and there is not very much anyone can do about stopping those acts. In the United States, even in spite of your covert operations and secrecy, there is strong support for your government to stand and state that these acts are not only illegal, but are going to be prosecuted. Often times in the Second and Third World, the government is not as effective as that.

Also, I saw freedom as a major component to peace. I knew there was hardly a chance of peace if I aligned with a country with its own history of terrorism. Then, when Jimmy Carter came into office, I saw a great chance to bring this peace plan into fruition.

I decided that the only way to force peace onto the area was to get into a position of power over our enemies. I raged the war in 1973 with the intent to bring them to their knees, and then offer them an olive branch. I felt strongly that this fight now had a different focus. I was not fighting for Allah, and some forgotten feud. I was fighting for an eventual end to the fighting.

The fact that I was positioned in time and place to make such a difference was an even more pressing point for me. What would you do if you were given the chance to possibly make peace out of an age-old conflict that has taken too many lives in its long history of killing? I guarantee you, you would add up your life, and realize, as I did, that, everyone dies someday. Why not risk that in order to change the world?

When I brought the Israelis to their knees, I looked into their eyes and saw them as children, with their mothers and fathers back home. I made myself think of them as humans living in a violent world, instead of the Great Enemy I was raised to hate. I regretted having to position myself in a way to "fight" for peace, but it was what was needed in the moment. From that place of advantage, I offered them an alternative.

Instead of bombing them, I offered them a new perspective. I began to rebuild our cities that were in range of our missiles, to make a statement about peace. This was at first a shock, and frankly, to both of us. Many of my ministers were dead set against this. They knew then, too, that I was writing my death sentence. They did not see eye-to-eye with me about bringing peace. To them, this was the "win" that the Arab world had waited for for so long.

But when I started talking with the Israelis, I became more and more excited about the prospect of bringing this act to the attention of the entire world. And now, here I was, also a friend to the United States, a friend of a friend of the Israelis, which was absolutely necessary to make this happen. Without the triad of countries, the United States as the peacemaking branch between the other two, none of this could have come about. I would have been killed a great deal sooner, I believe, had I not had the United States working with me.

How can I tell you what it was like to arrive at the Israeli airport years later? To see in the faces of people who for centuries were depicted as my enemies, now standing and cheering my arrival. My heart, in that moment, was perhaps as full as it has ever been. I knew then that I was right, that these mothers and fathers were tired of sending their children off to war, to die at the hands of the enemy. I knew they felt, as I did, that we were all family, brothers in the end, humans first and foremost.

Of course, there was dissension in the cabinet of Israel, too. I knew that, but the ministers we were working with were just as excited about the prospect of truly being able to stop the fighting. We talked over coffee at conference tables as fathers. We talked about how even we had to worry about our children being sent off the war, or being killed by terrorist action, or being taken by unfaithful governments. We talked as fathers, mostly, and for the first time, at least since I had been in power, we came to an understanding that surpassed the politics of our history.

That was all well and good, but we also knew that this was not just a matter of jolly conversation and affirming handshakes. We were suggesting rewriting the terms of culture. We needed to find practical ways to deal with the seemingly unsolvable problem of the Palestinians living in and around Jerusalem. As we sat to tackle this great challenge, some of the shine began to wear off.

In all my contemplation of peace, I did not stop to truly imagine how it would specifically take place. I knew we must work through the issues of the conflict, but little did I understand the logistics, including the economic and geographic problems of resolution. Before I became a peacemaker, the answer was simple: take back the land. During war, it was all or nothing. Now, I had to sit at a table and compromise, knowing that many in the Arab nation would have many different opinions of how this plan should look. There was not much chance of pleasing all of the Arab people. I knew I could deliver a separating blow to the Arab world if I compromised too much.

In the end, it was the Israelis who showed their deep understanding of the complexities, and agreed to allow self-rule in the West Bank and Gaza. They, too, knew that the hard line orthodoxy in their country would not support this, and yet, they knew they had no choice. There were many talks, and yes, some were heated and frustrating, about the rhetorical religious differences between the Arabs and Israelis. The Israelis believed they were chosen to come here and had a right to occupy this land. It had, after all, been given to them specifically after World War II. The Palestinians also believed that since they had been here since time forgotten, that they, too, had a right.

We who were negotiating knew, as men of standards, that if it were the roomful of us living in the Gaza, we would be able to successfully turn the land back to the self-rule. We knew, in order to live together, we would have to be respectful of each other's sovereignty and boundaries. But we also knew, sadly, that this might not be the case with many of the people who presently lived there, and much of the rest of the Arab-Israeli world.

But what else could we do? We knew we were making history, and we had to decide. As a statement, we knew Menachem's visit to Egypt would help solidify the factions of Israel that would follow his lead of peace.

That was all we could hope to do: solidify as much of the world as we could, and hope that, in time, our statement of learning to live together would carry on. Even if I did not live to see freedom and peace spread throughout the world, I knew that Allah had picked me to stand in this place, in this moment in time, and inspire the world to want peace.

By the time we got to Camp David, so much had already been talked about. We needed to settle in and see if we could iron out as many of the possible difficulties as we could. That time at Camp David was very special to me. It was a time of great privacy and reflection. We knew we would be remembered through the ages for those few weeks together.

Picture these three men of great world power, gathered at a retreat. An Arab, a Jew and a Baptist. Doesn't that strike you as symbolic? We worked with our aides and diplomats and writers during the day, and in the evening, we three would gather alone, over brandy and cigars, and speak with great affection for what we were all agreeing to do.

There was also a kind of fated reverence, for we all thought that any one of us could be assassinated by what we were doing. But talking about it openly with Jimmy and Menachem made it seem unimportant. I think perhaps the best work was done after hours.

With the United Nations having finished the conference, and the three of us with the Camp David Accords, it was over. We had molded a peace plan that we hoped would carry around the world, and serve as a model for other countries to follow. We wanted most to show the world that we could put aside our differences for the sake of the generations to come, to be able to teach our children through example that, yes, we can all love our own idea of God and still live peacefully together.

Q: Now that you see what has been happening in the world, particularly what has been happening in Egypt in the 1990s, are you disillusioned? It doesn't seem much better than when you lived.

AS: As far as Egypt goes, yes, it is very sad to see the changes that have swept through North Africa, and the terrorism that continues to rule there. At first glance, it would seem our peace plan had no effect at all on that world.

And still, I look upon this time you are living in as very exciting. You cannot forget that you have achieved peace in many countries that were former Soviet bloc countries. The wall coming down in Germany is perhaps one of the most magnificent achievements of peace and unity of the century. The fall of the former Soviet Union, while leaving economic destruction in its wake, was also a major factor of breaking up the stronghold that the USSR had, especially in the Middle East.

I see these times as times of great hope. The idea of peace is spreading far and wide. The idea of mothers and fathers standing up and demanding no more shedding of children's blood is much more understandable and applicable now.

Q: What are some of the challenges we are faced with as peacemakers in the new millennium?

AS: One of the greatest difficulties I see you having to

face is the great complexity of how to dismantle the war machines that so much of the world's economy is built on. Your military owns billions of dollars worth of weapons of war. They have factories within cities that house military personnel. You cannot just achieve peace without considering what to do about the present economic focus. You will need to find ways to transfer all that manpower and those resource over to something else that will sustain the families of military people.

Also, within your country right now is a great debate about guns. There is a civil war going on in the West. It has to do with the right to bear arms. Understand, those in the Middle East have always had free access to weapons. The idea that you in the West have considered making that illegal is a difficult cultural issue. You have created, with that, a conflict on a conflict: Do you think if you take away their weapons, they will automatically become peace-loving people? Those of you who own no weapons understand, it's not about the guns.

Those people who cling to the outmoded idea that weapons will protect them will be the hardest to win over to the peace process. Weapons will kill, that is their purpose. If you kill, you become a killer and fall to the enemy as much as if you had been killed. Had I thought that being assassinated was not an option, I would not have even tried to bring peace. Had my main concern been not to be killed, I would have had to continue to wage war.

I have killed a great deal in my life, indirectly. Just because I did not pull the actual triggers of all of the actual guns that killed does not absolve me of responsibility. Because I knew innately what I had to do, I chose to risk being killed rather than be the one who killed any more.

Perhaps the most difficult challenge will be to reach the individuals who believe so strongly in an eye-for-an-eye. In the Middle East, there is such a projection about fear of losing identity. This is not without merit, as our lands have fallen into the hands of foreigners, and some see the influence of the West as a dilution of the true tradition of culture of the Middle East.

There must be a way to inspire people to shift their focus from fear of losing identity to the joy of celebrating the diversity. Jews and Arabs can learn from each other. They can live together, still ensconced in their traditions and age-old personas, if they can learn to have respect for those traditions in others as well.

Beirut was a classic example of this kind of cooperation. For a time, in the '40s and '50s, Beirut was a place of great excitement, a melding of both the traditions and beliefs of the Middle East and the excitement of the new ideas from the West. It was a garden city, spawning poets and writers, new political thinking, a place of peace, much different than it is now. Although she is returning some to that time, she still is a very violent place.

People must learn to honor their own sovereignty so they will not be threatened by other cultures. The truth is, this world is becoming smaller and smaller. The challenge is to maintain the very rich and diverse cultures while blending them as well, bringing them together to live under one banner, the banner of peace.

Q: How did you move toward peace while in such a violent atmosphere?

AS: I built my first support around those who understood what peace was about, on a human level. Instead of trying to turn the heads of those who were instigators of the fighting, I looked to those who wanted to find the solutions and worked to solidify them. Then I presented the case to the next level of participants, that of the moderate Arabs. With what I could coalesce with them, I wanted to then approach the Soviets and their allies in the region. All the while I launched a rallying cry, through media, to draw into these circles as many people committed to peace as was possible.

Q: What can we do, as average citizens, to make peace a reality?

AS: You have a perfect opportunity in your culture today to take up this rallying cry. Between books, television, movies, music, and the Internet, your modern culture in the West has so many places for messages of peace. Try to infiltrate your culture in every way that you can, including your own conversations. Really intend to make a difference.

Appeal to the mothers and the fathers of all cultures. Try to understand, not the governments and politics of peace, but the men and women who live with the fear of their children being killed. Talk to the mothers in Northern Ireland and the fathers in Yugoslavia. Speak to the hearts of the Arab men and Chinese women. If you strip away the uniforms and religious rhetoric, and ask how they would feel about their children being killed in a war, you will find the heart of a pacifist.

Find a way to begin touching all those hearts. Start

with your own. Make your own daily commitment to peace. Dream as large as you can. Remember, I saw my own peace plan for a very long time before I was able to implement it. Don't allow yourselves to be daunted by realism. Know there is almost an impossible cry to your mission, just as I did. Know you might even be putting yourself in the face of danger to push the peace process.

I lived actually longer than I expected. I lived long enough to see the beginning stages of our plan. There are many who have died in the Arab-Israeli wars that never got to see their children grow up only to die in the next war. I feel incredibly lucky to have been who I was, and to have been such an important part of this peace movement as I was. And now I can see, despite the still-present atmosphere of violence, it does live on after I did. That was my only hope.

Q: Mr. Sadat, you mentioned that we couldn't just have this pie-in-the-sky idea of peace without looking at the economics of it. Is there really a way to turn the focus of all the resources of the military into peacemaking activities that will support the country the way that it did before?

AS: There is always a way if there is a will. But what else can you believe? How will it serve you to *not* believe that?

But are you asking is it easy? No, this is going to be a very difficult change. It won't be supported by everyone. You will be fought every step of the way. The complexity of the economics of transferring your focus to peace will be daunting at times.

If you begin to examine the dominoes that will fall, you will see how everything is so connected. The economics of ending war will require that all the mechanisms of war be transferred to a different focus. Perhaps all of the military bases will have to be adapted to become factories of different sorts. What kind of creative and needed industries could be applied to the workforce and resources?

Philosophically, the cultures of both the West and the Middle East will have to implement an entirely new focus to resolve conflicts. There are ancient religious belief systems that have been in place for many, many years, including Christianity, that will have to be rejuvenated to teach peace as a primary motive. This is not going to be an easy readjustment to the thousands of years of war-minded thinking, particularly within the Arab states.

But what you have on your side are bright, inspired, creative people working with mass, instant, global communications at their fingertips. What you can do in a day on the Internet would have taken years during my time, and could not have been accessible to the average citizen.

You must be asking yourself every day, "What can I do to promote peace on the grass roots level?" To begin with, talk about the possibility of peace. If you never promote conversation of ideas, you may never find the solutions to some of the difficult problems with which you are faced.

Organize on grass roots level all over the world through your Internet. Find ways to bring these different factions of peacemakers together, whether it be talking with someone down the street from you or working in the areas of politics and economics. Look for ways that you might not see at first. For example, working towards electric cars or mass transit will reduce the dependency on foreign oil. That lessens the economic power base of the ruling classes and the intention to use that power in armed conflicts.

Then, as you bring the grass roots factions together, you can use that power to influence those in power to see that the world really does want peace. Make your presence known, bring the power in your numbers and present that to the leaders, especially in the United States. Your democracy allows the openness and freedom to undertake this kind of organization without the imminent threat of terrorism to you or your family.

Become leaders. Get creative. Motivate yourselves. And perhaps most importantly, look at yourselves, and solve your conflicts on a personal level. Becoming a peacemaker is something everyone can do, for who doesn't have conflict in their lives? Study new ways of approaching the roots of conflict.

Early on, when I studied the Arab-Israeli conflicts throughout history, I could not get to a root. But in this day and age, you can begin to see the roots of where your conflicts lie. This refocused attention on your own personal power will help to promote less finger-pointing and more responsible action. Such a great gift, to be able to resolve your own conflicts.

The United States is the country that will lead this movement in the years ahead. Ordinary people will be rising from the ranks to lead this movement. If I can serve as an inspiration to anyone to make those steps towards peace, then my work in life was not in vain.

Jesus of Nazareth

Birth & Death Date Unknown

Manifestation, Self-Love & Heaven on Earth

Q: Jesus, you were considered to be both the Son of Man and the Son of God. Perhaps we could begin with you telling us, what was your life like as Jesus the Man?

JofN: Ah, yes, Jesus the Man. I enjoy that you're capitalizing "Man" and not just "God."

Perhaps the most relevant idea to start with is that Jesus the Man was exactly like any other ordinary person walking around on the Earth today. As a man, I felt every emotion, I bled when someone cut me, I had a strong attachment to my mother, I grew into an adult who was taken with a passion for a message and followed that passion right up to my death. Very little in my day-to-day activity would distinguish me from any of the other people around me, except for two things.

One was that I had this exceptional aura. A light actually emanated from within me. Sometimes my party of twelve would kid me about it, especially after sundown.

The other thing was, I was preternaturally detached from the details of my life. Very little would trigger me emotionally. Yes, there were times when getting upset served to deliver a message, like when I was dealing with the money changers in the temple. But those events didn't take place often. I didn't often use any emotion except love to get my message across.

Not that I didn't feel my emotions; I felt every emotion totally, deeply and completely. But I didn't attach a meaning for my feelings to the outside events in my life. My emotions kept the Son of Man grounded in the Son of God.

Q: Please talk about your original "Party of Twelve," the apostles.

JofN: My Party of Twelve was a well-organized and well-matched group of twelve men who represented different perspectives of humanity. They possessed among them all the conditions necessary to be present to support the manifestation of a complete human life. They were, in essence, representative of twelve elements that human spirit must possess in order to become a human life.

It would have been completely impossible for me to accomplish what I set out to do without their participation. I could not have done this alone.

One of their most important roles was to direct me through the details of my life. Because I was so detached from the details, my personal focus was usually on deeper matters concerning manifestation of physical form. I personally spent no energy in a day organizing events. That was left to the disciples. Of course, they would consult me, and my seemingly non-caring attitude of whether we should go to Canaan or to Galilee indicated to them that they were free to make those decisions.

What always amazed them was how, no matter where they sent me, something big happened. And things kept getting bigger and bigger. That was my intention. Being so detached, I had utmost faith that, however the details appeared, they would be perfect for my soul's manifest destiny, which was to bring a language and knowledge of human compassion onto the planet.

Having a group of twelve supporters to rely on through my passion was truly a master stroke of genius on the part of the organizing power.

Q: What exactly do you mean, "organizing power?"

JofN: I mean God. From God's mind emanates a master plan. Imagine if you can that there are at least as many elements of the master plan as there are human beings. In truth, there are infinite possibilities for every one of those human beings as well. This giant mechanism of energy, manifested as billions of people on this planet Earth, in a solar system filled with infinite celestial bodies, co-created by and existing for humanity to learn how to become pure compassion in human form, this is what you consider to be God.

Q: So God as a "He" doesn't exist?

JofN: No, not in a singular form. It was a great challenge to translate this into the political and spiritual language of the times. I spoke in parable for that reason: to frame the complex scientific understandings in basic, day-to-day metaphors that ordinary people could understand. I spoke of the Mother and the Father because everyone could understand those terms personally. I talked about God's family to present a reference point of everyone being of the Tribe of Humanity.

I purposefully caused great controversy that got the world's attention. With the help of my party of twelve, the message carried throughout the fear-based infrastructure of humanity, amassing through time, changing directions and meaning, eventually making its way into written form, to be edited and deleted and restructured into the bibles of today.

Did I speak in terms of God as an energy in the culture of the day that was beyond scientific understanding? I did. There were several groups of people with whom I could discuss these things, some of whom were Greek. We also discussed out-of-body experiences, materialization and dematerialization, and many other things that weren't necessarily for the mainstream people of that time. Believe it or not, many people did not look upon me as the Messiah.

Q: So, in essence, we are all God.

JofN: Yes, every human being channels the God-energy. It is literally impossible to be alive without it.

Adolph created a position of the complete absence of light, manifest in human form in the physical world. I manifested into physical form the presence of everything divine. Both of us have been absolutely essential to bringing humanity to complete understanding of its spiritual nature. All of us, together, are God.

God manifests into physical human form to learn to harness the power of this duality using free will choices to decide to create heaven on Earth. Therefore, the Jesus in you must meet the Hitler in you, and come to non-judgmental terms with the ramifications of both. This requires the ability to forgive.

In the end, it will be Adolph who really teaches you how to forgive.

Q: Did you reincarnate like Einstein explained, into just one life, into the life of Jesus of Nazareth, over and over again?

JofN: Yes, absolutely. I reincarnated into the life of

Jesus the Man at least twenty-seven different occasions, each life with a different arrival and departure time, varying lengths and details unique unto each and every life. After while, I began to see through the fabric of physical existence, while I was still in it. I saw the energetic side of everything, every moment, every part of the dance of the human life that I lived.

I wasn't any more divine than anyone else. I volunteered and was chosen to focus strictly on the manifestation of love. Like you, I was offered an incredible opportunity to advance myself. What can I say? I ran with it.

As an infinite spirit, I reincarnated all of my energy into the life that was Jesus of Nazareth, over and over again. In each life, I made different decisions and studied where the various paths took me. Each life ended in a different way, and the effect of the different lives on the rest of world and through time was equally varied. In one life, I lived to a ripe old age, with grandchildren and great-grandchildren, but my influence did not reach through time like it did when I was a public teacher who was then crucified.

The life I lived as the tentmaker reached around the countryside. On its own, it wasn't able to affect people in the 1990s as much as the life of the crucified teacher. But, oh, how I loved to make tents! And travel, and talk. I talked to so many people, and the tentmaker had the same agenda as the crucified teacher: how to live in peace, together, as one family, the Tribe of Humans.

There was also another crucifixion. In one life as a common criminal, I was also crucified. Another life brought me much happiness with a beautiful wife and family. In another, I was a great doctor, where many of the stories of the physical healings originated.

As an emissary of God, I came to show humans how to choose love. My entire agenda in every life had to do with the manifestation of pure love. Even in the life as the criminal, my agenda was still that of teaching love. Only one of those lives reached through time, and all around the world.

The ultimate goal was to create a life of such consciousness that I could see past the illusion of dying. I knew I had died infinite times already. My God-mind completely understood where I had come from. But I needed my Man-mind and physical body to understand that, too, while I was in human form.

Believe it or not, I appeared to people in every life after my every death. In those Hebrew times, it was considered something shameful and unclean to deal with the dead in any way. Not many people spoke of it openly. So, after the tentmaker's death when I appeared to my mother, she just thought she was seeing a longed-for image of her dead son.

Slowly but surely, the details of each life began to bleed through time and space onto one another. There were so many lives and stories. Eventually, my heart was so full, my mind so unaffected by the illusions of physical reality, my body living in this super dimensional perception, I was able to create the perfect life to take this message through time and effect a change in the actual infrastructure of human existence.

The same people reappeared again and again, in life after life, performing a different role in each life. Someone who had been my best friend in one life was the solider who nailed me to the cross in the next. It was truly a multi-leveled chessboard of creation.

The one thread that ran through all my lives was that no matter who I was—tentmaker, doctor, grandfather, carpenter, criminal—I was always just an ordinary person.

Q: Can you explain a little about the virgin birth?

JofN: One of the reasons it's called the virgin birth, by the way, is because it was the first time one of us actually created life, bypassing the fear-based rules that would normally dictate the actions of conception.

I knew as I approached this high level of awareness of what I was capable of creating, that I had to birth one brilliant life that would be remembered throughout time. It had to encompass all of my works, all of the fruits of living all of those other lives. I needed both the agony and the ecstasy to make this lasting mark. I needed something dramatic enough to be talked about through time.

When Mary and I decided I would be born without her union with a man, that instead we would just use the power of our own completion to manifest my fetus, we knew what the world would think. She knew she did not have sex with Joseph. No one could take that knowledge away from her, no matter what they thought. But few understood the real meaning of that series of events.

Working with Mary on an energetic level, we created through the power of our own manifestation, my fetus, without Joseph's sperm. It was a most magnificent event. Although Mary's conscious mind was hidden in the fear-based infrastructure, energetically she knew the great accomplishment that had taken place. The angels visited her conscious mind in physical form to help her remember just enough to verify the outcome. We had successfully instigated my own conception through the amassing of divine consciousness in our human forms. I discovered how to pass into physical form through the birthright of self-creation.

We decided to send messengers ahead with omens, to herald the truth of this amazing feat. Sending angels and spreading the word about the virgin birth was the best way we could leave what you might call a "paper trail."

Within this 2,000-year era of Christianity that has held a firm grip on conscious thinking, not many others have come forward claiming to have self-created their own fetus, but others have. Indeed.

Q: Was Mary your mother in every life?

JofN: Truth be told, the real power of the story behind Jesus of Nazareth lies in the story of his mother. Her anguish is perhaps even more important than my crucifixion. This pain has allowed her to endure as long as she has through time and in the hearts of so many.

Her consistency in reincarnating as my mother allowed her to experience the same level of perception I achieved. Throughout all our lives together, her representation of the ultimate mother gifted her with a presence that surpasses all understanding. As holder of the indispensable seed of compassion, it was vital that she returned to influence, as I have.

Q: Tell us about the political atmosphere of where you grew up. You, like Anwar, experienced the Arab-Israeli tensions even back then.

JofN: The region in the time I chose to live was aligned to Rome and the caesars vying to conquer as much of the world's people as they could. Colonialism was alive and well then, too, steeped with segregation. It wasn't just the Arabs and Israelis. Many laws of the class systems, rules, and religious practices served to separate people into one sect or another. Unity was often done to power rebellion, not to create one family sharing the Earth.

The details of the problems that the Middle East faces today may not be the same as they were back then, but the same condition exists: each sect taking exorbitant pride in their perspective of life. Those seeking outside validation through associations to these sects actually create separation, one human apart from another, thereby creating separatist thinking as well. This, by nature, creates conflict.

This separatist thinking has easily permeated the Middle East because each different sect has an outside standard-bearer, an idol or master, if you will, who is perceived as somehow better and more powerful than the masses. Instead of teaching people to access their own voices of authority from within, the sects create a set of guidelines which the followers must believe in order to be a part of the sect. Playing off the religionists' need for outside validation, these guidelines are fear-based, and make assumptions that those who don't adhere to these guidelines are in some way "wrong." That then becomes a reason for becoming the aggressors. Fighting for what is perceived as "right" through the filter of the fear-based guidelines, the sects each find reasons to justify fighting the other. This is how Holy Wars are born.

The Arabs and Israelis have truly indeed forgotten that they are of the same tribe. In the roots of that region lie the birthplace of much of humankind. Imagine upholding a lifelong feud with your neighbor that stretches before you can remember, with gruesome stories handed down generation to generation that convince you to carry on the fighting, then discovering your neighbor's great-grandfather was second cousin to your great-grandmother. How does it feel to discover you are actually from the same blood?

Q: What then are the roots of this livelong feud in the Middle East? Mr. al-Sadat said he tried to find the origins of it and couldn't.

JofN: Structures of government, religions, politics, most all organizations of associations were built around a primal sense of fear. Because of this, your culture has a fear-based infrastructure. Quite simply, the fear borne of suddenly awakening in this harsh, unknown environment is the root of all fear within humanity.

To understand, you must go back to the beginning of the human consciousness. Picture a large tribe of newly-emerging people, learning to live together, acquainting themselves with the environment, fighting for their lives against the elements. The major condition dominating their instincts is fear: fear of the environment, fear of the unknown, fear of darkness, fear of light such as fire and lightening, fear of annihilation.

Within this emerging human was installed a heart, to feel, to mourn, to celebrate, to laugh, to be divinely connected to the inner source. Emotions were intended to be each individual's one-to-one connection to his or her divine life. Emotions were also the great equalizer. Everyone in the tribe received the capability to feel, and conversely, the capability to deny those feelings.

Also installed in the new human was an intellect, or sometimes called an ego. This ability to define perception was meant to equip these new humans with a kind of sonar system. As their new bodies picked up information on a primal, instinctual level, messages were then sent to the ego, a series of descriptions of what was happening, meant as an inner compass and to communicate with other members of the tribe.

As the intellect began to define what it was perceiving, these newborn creatures of consciousness started to organize, much like cellular activity on a molecular level. Different members of the tribe began to identify with one element outside themselves or another. At first, they gravitated toward nature's elements: wind, water, wood or fire. This division amongst the tribe was meant to develop diversity. From the infrastructure of fear, however, it also became about separatism.

Nature soon gave way to thought, and thought's ability to conquer nature. This brought symbols with which to identify. Flags, emblems, coats of arms, grails, all were outward symbols to rally under in kinship. These evolved into associative language coalitions: people attracting and gathering because of similar definitions of what they were perceiving. Those who were afraid of lightening and believed it was the wrath of an angry God rallied together. They separated themselves from those who took a more natural meaning. The differences were sometimes celebrated and embraced, but more often than not, it became about which one was the "right" point of view.

One type of associative language group was religion. Each different religious affiliation believed that their god was the "right" God. They built temples to their god as a form of worshipping those they perceived had a greater power than they themselves could ever hope to have.

Within the different religious groups there emerged

certain people who could scribe God's words. These prophets were separated from the rest of the tribe as people who had special powers to talk directly to God. The rest of the group then began to listen to the words of the scribe instead of listening to their own connection to these inner voices. No one realized that the words from the scribe were available to everyone in the tribe. In this way, separation from self began to take place within the individuals of the separatist groups.

The natural birthright of every human being is a one-to-one connection to their God within. God speaks to everyone, every day. Having the voice of God within is an indivisible part of being human. Part of the challenge you are faced with as a civilization is to come to an understanding of the billion different ways God speaks to the planet.

Now, the Arabs, gathering and attracted by stories from their beloved ancestors, held certain beliefs about the Israelis, and used the definitions of those beliefs to keep the Israelis away. All of the stories were based in fear: fear that the Israelis, who appeared to be so foreign and unattractive, were somehow dangerous to the Arab group identity. The Israelis did the same.

Born of fear and disconnected from the words of love within them, each set of separatists projected their fear onto the opposing group, and framed their definitions in ways that made it look like each group opposed the other's ideals, thereby giving them each a justifiable reason to fight against one another. Deeper and deeper the chasm became, until each side has carried on their own cycle of projection and separatism to the point of possible complete annihilation of the entire planet Earth.

What you don't understand is, first, you are all one tribe, and second, the only thing you can be separated from is yourself.

Q: Are you also referring to Christianity?

JofN: Yes, I am referring to Christianity as a body of work that's represented in my name. I need to state now, I am not a Christian. Does that strike you as odd? Perhaps not.

I worked in my life to educate and inspire people to look within for the source of their own power. My message carried the innocence of a child: love yourself well, and then love your neighbor in the same way. Live every day with this covenant of self-love, and project that love over everyone you meet. I spoke out in every life, at every stop, with everyone from commoners to religious leaders. I loved everyone as an equal. I loved myself, teaching through living example, knowing that if I didn't love myself, I'd be incapable of loving others. I worked many lifetimes to bring this message of peace.

Through the centuries, all sorts of definitions have arisen in the interpretation of my messages. People have taken my message of self-love, filtered it through this infrastructure of fear, and are now using it to prove how defective they are. They hold up an ideal model in the form of Jesus Christ, and compare themselves to that outward model. Instead of learning to tap into the power within, as I did, they make idols of my body and claim that it was I who came to save them from being evil. By looking to me as the source of their salvation, they are diverting their attention once again outside themselves, completely losing sight of my message. In an effort to prove their separateness, they twist my words of self-love around to support their positions of fear, judgment and intolerance.

I must emphatically state: It was never my intention that anyone "worship" me. When I said, "I am the way, the truth and the light," I was referring to the " I AM" that each individual human is also. So, it is *you* who say to yourself, "*I* am the way, the truth and the light." Look within to find your divinity, to become the human embodiment of love. Don't look at me and claim that I am the only one who can accomplish this level of divinity manifest in human form. I told you over and over again, what I can do, so can you.

Most of you are not aware of the illogical thinking being evoked by your fear. You say you believe I died for your sins, and all you have to do is think that and you will be saved. And yet you still look upon yourself as a "sinner." If I had indeed come to die for your sins, then, logically, there can be no more sinners!

If you continue to look outside yourself for the source of your own divinity, you will continue to perpetuate the fear-based infrastructure.

Two thousand years later, I have a personal opportunity to set the world straight. To speak up once again and dispel the mythology, the cruelty and the illusion that the fear and separation have created.

That is why I created the concept of the Second Coming. So I can now speak again. Assuredly, if you had experienced this misinterpretation of your message of self-love, you, too, would want to return and speak.

Q: So is that why you are speaking with us now?

JofN: In part, and in part to dispel the myth that I am somehow closer to God than anyone else. Yes, I succeeded in manifesting a destiny of peace, and came to a complete understanding of the nature of myself while in physical body, but that doesn't make me intrinsically more divine than anyone else. That only makes me more well-rehearsed.

There was a reason I wasn't born a king, like everyone expected. I was supposed to be ordinary because everyone is ordinary. Ordinary people can use their power to do what I did. Everyone. Every Arab, every Englishman, every Israeli, every Sri Lankan, everyone is ordinary and everyone can do what I did.

Each human on the planet is a part of a universal truth: All humans need clean water to drink, fresh air to breath and food to eat to nourish the body, the human vessel of God. This is the world of humanity. Thus is the cycle of life.

Humanity is the one tribe from which we have all descended. This, and self-love, is all you need to know. Everything other than that is a construct of fear.

Q: But you came to teach the lessons of unconditional love, and self-love. That was not based on fear.

JofN: Yes, but I came to teach this not as a religion, but as an action, a decision. I came to implore all people to make decisions in love. I did not come to organize people around fear-based associations, but I knew that would happen. I knew before I came into the incarnation of crucified teacher that I was coming into a fear-based society and, paradoxically, that this fear was going to be part of what kept my message growing in that life, and alive for all these years.

Q: Then why did you come if you knew what fear would do to your message?

JofN: For that very reason. I had to come and infiltrate the fear-based infrastructure. I came to present a new plan to create a love-based infrastructure through choice and free will. The job of Jesus of Nazareth, the crucified teacher, was to infiltrate his culture so thoroughly that his story would live on through time, as long as it could, until there came a time when everyone understood the new infrastructure completely. I came to plant the seeds of transformation that would begin the changes in the infrastructure. This transformation was about substituting love for fear within the creation of systems on Earth. And the only way I could do that was to become love in the center of the fear. The same holds true for all of you.

Don't be fooled by the apparent state of the modern world. It's not a great deal more violent than it was when I was on the planet. Only today violence can have a much farther reach. But one-to-one violence, terrorism, murder, rape, capital punishment, all were very real in my day.

Q: I have to make one comment at this point. Jesus, you sound much more like a scientist than the Son of God.

JofN: I felt more like a science teacher than a holy man. A paradox indeed.

My teachings stress that I came to teach you how to do what I do, not save you from yourself. Only you can make the choices that save you from yourself.

Everyone has this divine access within them, and I

came to show you how to access that divinity and the birthright of eternal life. I came to show that it's humanly possible not only to look past the infrastructure built on cycles of fear, but to actually create a new one based on love, on pure compassion. That love is a by-product of the decisions that you make; it's not a product of an association or an intellectual definition. Love and its birthright are much more scientific than they are moralistic.

Look at it this way: The nature of life is to re-create itself. Creation is regeneration. It's the birthright of every particle of light, of sound, of energy, of spirit to recreate itself. The entire regenerative nature of life is within you.

The infrastructure of fear is degenerative. This permeates your molecular level in such a way that creates a complete paradox. On one hand, your birthright is to create yourself again and again, and yet, every environment you create yourself into begins to decay the life you created. From this conflict, on this molecular level, comes all the conflicts that manifest in the world.

So, yes, every world war, every neighbor murdered, every child abused, every sickness, everything that is violent and destructive and filled with fear emanates from the center of this paradox.

Q: So you came to help us overcome our fears? If we could, what would happen? Would we somehow change the very basis of our molecular structure?

JofN: Yes. You change the infrastructure. You would create Heaven on Earth.

Q: But how do we do that? Just by loving ourselves?

JofN: "Just?" You say this as if it's a mere thought mentioned or name dropped.

Q: Okay, then, could you define "compassion?"

JofN: Compassion is choosing to nurture a non-judgmental relationship with life. It's making a choice to remove judgment, and then acting from an intention of divinity, or to do the highest good for all involved. This is complete and total unconditional love.

Each time you choose love, you affect a change in the fear-based infrastructure from a molecular level. You only perceive the intellectual changes, or changes in your attitude, and don't associate that change as having any affect on a molecular level. But all of the physical life you perceive is created with particles from that molecular level. Physical form, thoughts, emotions, spirit, all are born of molecular activity. That molecular energy is your source for life on Earth.

So, yes, when you make a decision to take an action in love instead of fear, you bring consciousness to another segment of the love-based infrastructure. You then project that love out over the world, just like you used to project fear. By projecting love, you also change the way you respond to fear projected onto you. You change the nature of the energy you are channeling into the world. You then channel love, creating and influencing everything in your path, becoming a walking example of how to live, instead of just talking about it, or waiting for someone else to show you love. At that point, you will stop talking about me doing it, and realize you are doing it yourself.

Q: Can we talk about your crucifixion?

JofN: Just like Adolph knew he was going to create hell on Earth, I knew my job was to convince people that Heaven still existed on Earth, that the Garden of Eden was a metaphor for Earth and each individual's birthright was one of creation. I also knew that the fear-based infrastructure was going to take the language of self-love and twist it into fear and hatred. That's exactly what happened, and what is still happening today.

The life of the crucified teacher culminated in the actualization of my ability to retain physical manifestation of my body after death. In those last cognitive moments on the cross, I transcended death. I seamlessly saw the passage from life in the physical body to death and return to spirit, without losing my physical form.

It was all remarkably seamless. My body never did actually die; I wouldn't allow it. They even tried to stab me to death, but nothing could kill it. They eventually just took it down and carried it to the tomb.

Because of the weight of my body against my lungs, I could not speak at the end. But at one point in the crucification, I was able to say, "Forgive them, Father, for they know not what they do." They certainly didn't understand the gift I received when I died on the cross in that life, and saw spirit as humanity and humanity as particles of spirit instantaneously fused. There was truly no separation in that moment. For the first time in all my lives, I achieved the conscious recognition of what I had been doing on a much greater level, from a much greater part of myself. For all of that, I wanted to thank everyone who had played a part in helping me make this profound realization while still in physical form.

Another one of the meanings of those powerful words came from my understanding of what the fear-based infrastructure was going to do with the event of my crucifixion. I knew humans would use this event to create destruction: first, the inner guilt about "murdering God," then the accusations of one religion against another, with punishment and judgments growing in the message. I also knew that people would mistakenly look at me as some kind of martyr, that my death as a common criminal on the cross would be seen as a sacrifice to save them.

What I didn't fully comprehend at the time was to what extent the message would be used against itself. Some people have come to believe that, in order for them to achieve what they call "eternal life," that they have to confess to believing that I really did die on the cross to "save" them from their sins. This simple confessional has become the cornerstone of an entire sect of Christianity. Again, by looking outside the self, they are destroying the very message I came to teach.

My mission has always been about one very simple thing: that self-love is the cornerstone of transforming the fear-based infrastructure. The act of turning your attention inward and connecting to that divine source of infinite life that dwells within, as your birthright, is the act of living in the awareness of eternal life. It's not about believing what I said, it's about doing what I did. To that end, you don't have to believe that turning your attention inward will change the infrastructure in order for that change to take place. Even if you didn't believe in the idea of self-love, if you practiced it, you would see the powerful effects it has. On the other hand, just believing that Jesus the Man/God died to save you from your sins once again throws your focus outward, losing the effect.

But no matter. Your eternal life is not based on belief in it. If you can't understand your eternal nature while living in this physical body, it will be there waiting for you after you pass away and return to the consciousness of pure energy. You all come back to the eternal place of spirit. Some will sleep for awhile, others will get right back to work, planning and negotiating and re-creating life. It goes on and on.

And it goes on and on for all people. Jews, Muslims, Baptists, Buddhists, Atheists, Aleuts, everyone everywhere as members of the Tribe of Humanity will die and come back to this place of spirit, to live on eternally, constantly creating more and more life, trying over and over to transform the infrastructure of the system.

Q: Do you think what people have done with your message is bad? People who use your words of love to bolster their positions of fear, are they working against all the work you did when you were in physical form?

JofN: They are only playing out the need for the infrastructure to change to love, starting from the source within each individual. They are revealing to themselves the very fear base they possess in order to make the decision to transform it to one of self-love.

They are not cursed. No one is cursed for choosing to come to life, no matter how foul-smelling and deceptive they may seem. All life is of God and about creation, even in its most unattractive and repulsive form.

Everything is made of particles of energy. The cohesive unit of the manifestation of spirit is matter, and creation of that is always a perfect process.

Perfection has two meanings. The perfection of coming to life in the first place is one thing. The cycle of creation and regeneration is a perfect process. There's life, and then there's death. They serve each other well, and are needed to re-create the process of creation. In that sense, everything is perfect.

Perfection as holding yourself up to an outside model is a different kind of perfection. That is based on fear, because it comes from outside self. Even with the most loving intentions of manifesting spirit, a belief system that takes your focus of power anywhere outside self is fear-based.

There are stories of me telling people to "fear God." How would you know what it was that I actually said with all these different interpretations of my words? The only way you would be able to truly understand what I was teaching would be to create within yourself an infrastructure of self-love, and then hold everything up to that inner model. All decisions and perspectives must be filtered through the model of that love-based infrastructure within in order for your creation to be love-aligned. It must start within yourself. You can use my example to inspire you, but you must create for yourself your own working model of an infrastructure of self-love.

When enough people create an infrastructure of love within themselves that connects to the one source of all love, then there will be no more fear-based filters. When you put out energy in love, it will be returned with the same energy. In this way it regenerates itself without having to be born and die and born again, because there is no more fear-based infrastructure to destroy it. It has now transformed that infrastructure and the rules that the infrastructure operates under as well.

Q: Would you tell us what "real love" is?

JofN: Real love is self-love. Every detail in your outer life is the reflection of your inner life. All of your relationships with friends and family are based on the quality of your inner life, on your relationship to yourself. If you possess a strong atmosphere of self-loving energy within, patience and compassion for yourself, it will reflect outside you in the form of regenerating love, love that does not destruct.

Q: Is there a kind of love that is destructive?

JofN: There is a form of love that is not entirely self-related. This is a kind of love that seeks outside of itself. What is meant by seeking outside of self is an infrastructure that perceives itself as needy, or flawed, as a sinner, and that someone or something other than self will transform that need or flaw. Since regenerative love is found within, seeking outside of self creates a structure based on illusion and deception. It is a lie against the science of how human spirit actually functions. It also removes your perceived ability to choose love for yourself.

Love that seeks outside itself will create, but it will not create regenerative relationships, situations or lessons. It will create only to be destroyed: a marriage started in love ending in fear; a belief system that begins in justice but ends in autocracy.

What most humans don't realize is that love is the substance of the creative force of the universe. Love is the urge of life to create. Because you were conceived in love, you bring with you into life the power of creation. Every decision you make decides the quality and energy of your life.

Even someone like Adolph Hitler created a life for himself. Due to the fear-filled nature of his inner life, he created destruction, but he created nonetheless. You see the challenges in coming to a perspective of complete non-judgment of the universe in its present state?

Q: So we shouldn't worship you as the savior. Are you saying that we are exactly like you, that we are God, too?

JofN: I certainly am. The only difference is timing. I came, fully conscious, to demonstrate how humans can reach a complete understanding of the true nature of reality and the power of the self. I never meant for you to hold me up as some icon of the divine. It was not my intention for you to twist the words of the love-based infrastructure to construct a reason for fighting and wars and separation.

And yet, in keeping with the paradox, I knew that was exactly what was going to happen. That's why it had to be a two-part initiative. I had to make use of the duality of life to bring my message home even more. That's why I intended the Second Coming.

Q: When you originally talked about the Second Coming, did you mean you would come back to Earth as a human again?

JofN: No. The Second Coming referred to a time in the future generations when people would be much more capable of comprehending self-love than the people in the times in which I had lived. I knew in the future I'd be able to facilitate communication through the inner life of spirit. I'd be able to personally speak to every human from their own connection to their inner spirit, just like Albert could be everywhere at once.

In my commitment to bringing a transformation to the infrastructure, I had to be prepared for you to work through the processing of this information for 2,000 years. That's why the story had to last throughout time. All the different sects of Christianity have passed the story down from generation to generation. Even some Jews are retelling the story of the Messiah with new metaphor. All the interpretations, motivations, understandings and depictions have stretched to infinite possibilities. My message has been used all over the world for every reason imaginable.

There is a built-in protection plan with love and creation. If you create chaos in your life, you will experience that chaos in spirit form after you die. Then, you are sanctioned to burn that chaos away as karma. Like Adolph, you spend a great deal of energy in the Afterlife processing the deep emotions and terror that came from the consequences of your actions, or you go on to create another life wherein the actions of your previous life come full circle in the next: you were murdered, you become the murderer.

Every life is designed to give you a piece of the deepest, most empowering perspective of pure compassion and to prepare you to create a life based on an infrastructure of perfect love.

The form of perfect I use here is about being so awake that you are no longer fooled or detained by the infrastructure of fear. You see clearly, while you're alive in physical body, exactly what lies beneath the physical in the particle form of energy. You know you are creating your life, and that when your physical body dies, your spirit will still exist and your inner gravity will reorganize itself to accommodate the demands of your regeneration. You fully realize that you have, as your birthright, eternal life.

When you reach that kind of knowing, you become detached from the details of life. No longer do you create anguish because you are no longer fooled into believing the fear-based infrastructure. You create clarity and compassion and single-mindedness. You then aren't afraid of dying for your cause, because you know there is no death. You aren't afraid of losing your body because you know it's just another manifestation of spirit, and that spirit is eternal. Eventually, like me, you will not have to experience death. You can see past even the illusion of physical death, and choose regeneration.

Q: Would you tell us more about compassion?

JofN: Compassion brings you deep into your own heart by removing all judgment and releasing yourself from the need to create destruction. It's the interface between the duality of the worlds. Compassion allows you to transcend the need to believe in the finite world, passing judgments and clinging to the illusion of three-dimensional reality.

Without compassion for yourself, you can never generate compassion for the world around you. As long as you hold fear in your hearts and project that fear outward into physical form, the more you will be trapped by the illusions of the details of your life.

Compassion allows you safe passage into the place of non-judgment. Non-judgment then allows you to experience the world from this detached state, taking in the creation of the moment, living with love in present moment, choosing to manifest in love instead of creating destruction from inner fear. This is the only way to pass into the kingdom of heaven while you are still in physical body. Compassion is the only way to see past the illusions of fear.

Q: What is heaven?

JofN: Heaven begins within, and is the conscious manifestation into physical form of the mirror image of one's own divinity as experienced from the place of pure spirit. It's not a place you go after you die; it's a physical state of consciousness. Your life as a human is in heaven.

The life force that creates you to think, to breathe, to eat, to love, to cry, that life force is a mysterious miracle. That life force is the energy of heaven, taking you with it into that place of total truth and realization, of complete compassion. That's why you are presently still in heaven.

But … it's nearly impossible to perceive this place of heaven from the infrastructure of fear. That doesn't mean you aren't still in heaven, still a being of supreme spirit, creating your life as you go. Just because your human mind doesn't believe you are that powerful doesn't mean that you aren't.

One of the main purposes of my messages of compassion was to teach people how powerful they are and inspire them to use that power to return to the truth that you live in heaven. Without compassion, personal power falls prey to the truth of the illusion, to the fear-based infrastructure.

When you take your first breath as a child, you are in a rare condition of being fully present in spirit and in body. In those moments before your human mind begins to align with the fear-based infrastructure, your being knows its true nature. For awhile, as a child, you are able to live with that complete knowing.

But very soon, fear takes over and moves to you separate from that knowledge. You are taught from an early age to be afraid of your personal power. You're told that because of the possibility that you might use that power destructively you should avoid using it at all. Because of this judgment you become afraid of what you might create, all the while unaware that you are creating the fear in the first place. Then, out of mistrust for yourself, you abdicate your power by following the authority of sources outside yourself.

Q: Do you think religions are dangerous because they encourage people to give up their power?

JofN: Dangerous might not be the right word. I believe they are controlling and keeping the fear-based infrastructure in place. This in and of itself is not a dangerous thing, any more than being alive through any civilization has been a dangerous thing.

Certainly great destruction has been generated from religious institutions and belief systems. Christianity is responsible for a great deal of the destruction of the world. But then, so is Islam and Judaism. Any religion that promotes the abdication of personal power and asks the believer to seek outside themselves for the answer is degenerative. This creates that self-destructive cycle wherein the believer does not find fulfillment because they are seeking outside themselves.

It is good to have a compassionate advisor, but you must claim that power of compassion as your own in order to create the regeneration you are seeking for fulfillment. You and you alone are responsible for each and every one of your personal decisions.

Q: Will we ever achieve world peace? And if so, how will we ever get the entire world to think this way?

JofN: Yes, you will come to remember heaven on Earth. That is the mission here. That has been the mission ever since humanity began to walk on the Earth: to remember that you are divine beings of both spirit and flesh.

In the story of Adam and Eve, when Adam ate the apple, he became aware of himself as a human, separate from Spirit. This evoked fear. This is the same fear that the baby feels as it leaves the womb of the mother, only to be blinded by the light of physical reality.

Fear not! Humans all over the world at this time are listening to my words. This is what the Second Coming is about: the Christ Consciousness being heard by each and every human, not just the Christians. It's a universal broadcast, aired in every language, about the true nature of human self. Many, many people around the world are listening and understanding. It's planting the seeds for a great event that will unify those people. It starts on a one-to-one platform and grows to encompass the entire world.

Yes, we will achieve world peace. No matter how many lifetimes, how much destruction, there will come a time when you will all learn this true nature while in physical body. I know it will happen because it is the destiny of heaven and spirit.

Not everyone will act at first. Those who stubbornly cling to the fear-based infrastructures will continue to create for themselves a hellish Earth, filled with destruction. They will continue learning on the levels that they need, but they will not be able to perceive heaven, for it is within, and they will be seeking outward.

Those who listen to the inward compassion and detach from the illusions of the outer world will discover the capability to choose to create this new perspective, this new world, this heaven on Earth. From this perspective, everything is of God.

Q: I've heard a theory that people will disappear off the Earth, hundreds of thousands at one time, and people who were dead will have their bodies again. Is this part of this?

JofN: Yes, while those in physical body are learning to see past the illusion of the physical world, those in spirit are continuing to experiment with the manifestation of creation. There is an entire soul group who has been infiltrating physical form using some of the information we gathered while creating the virgin birth.

My life went on to be about manifestation. I materialized the substance of the grapes into the water jugs, and then manifested the process of turning it into wine; I drew into our nets fish, and bread into our baskets to feed the hungry. Those things were already possible in the physical world; I just reached past the illusion of separation and made them happen at light speed. I was not creating a new set of rules: I was merely working on a different time/space continuum using the very rules of physical manifestation.

So, yes, there will be people who create a different life for themselves without having to enter again down the birth canal as a helpless baby. Instead of waiting for two other humans to participate in the form of mother and father, they will manifest themselves a physical body. They might choose to be fully grown, or a child, in Spain, or South Africa. They will see past the illusion and work on a molecular level to create life. The possibilities are endless when you detach with compassion, and see the true nature of yourself.

Then, those who still look outward will only see the physical manifestation of their own fear. They will not be able to see you, seated in compassion, because you are going to manifest a world based on the truth of heaven on Earth.

On that Earth, there will be no more wars. Humans will not murder other humans, children will not die of AIDS or be persecuted, discriminated against or abused. It truly will be heaven on Earth.

Q: How can we ordinary people work towards world peace? Is there something we're missing here? The world seems to only be getting more violent.

JofN: The only thing you are missing is when you choose not to look inward for the divine source of your own creation energy. Once you learn to consciously use your divine inner energy, your birthright of creation, peace becomes the by-product of the act of looking inward and honoring yourself as holy, too. Don't worry about how it will manifest on the planet. Like karma, the world outside you will be based on what you are creating within.

Education is a great inspirer. That was what I devoted myself to in the final years of my life. I committed my life to spreading the word of looking inward, to understanding the kingdom of heaven is within, and is your birthright.

The best work you can do is to look inward. Open your heart to being committed to compassion. Come to understand why the very act of choosing non-judgment is so transformative. Serve as a beacon for others to create a love-based infrastructure. Try to understand those who are fear-based and how you can best help them switch their focus gently inward.

This is a great challenge, especially for the old guards of the ancient realms, who feel that opening to self-love will annihilate them. The case of the Arab-Israeli conflict is one of the oldest organized guards in world history. This feud stretches back to the beginning of recorded history.

It is time for a new honor roll to be called. It is time to call upon every individual, regardless of race, of color, of creed or order, to look inward upon themselves and see what energy they are giving out to the world. This means everyone: every Arab, every Jew, every Christian … every one a member of the Tribe of Humanity, living together on the planet Earth.

As you begin to look inward, quickly you become inspired. Now you're regenerating your energy, not destroying it. You're building up energy. What are you going to do with all that energy now that it's you aren't self-destructing? That energy is your pallet, your canvas and your song.

You have been called here to sing your human body to life in order to create a new time of peace and understanding, of unity all across the world. You are here to make sure that everyone receives proper food, has clean water to drink and fresh air to breathe, and rich soil in which to sink roots.

You are here, each and every one of you, to become a vessel for pure compassion. That is all. Be surprised by whatever follows after that.

Many of us here in the Afterlife have been trying to inspire individuals on Earth to come together and make a brilliant statement that will shine through the present circumstances of your planet. One such incident was a group of men who gathered in Copenhagen in 1997 with the intention to commit to a new idea of peace in the Middle East. Many of us were with them in spirit. Myself, Anwar, Albert, and Sigmund, we all did our parts behind the scenes of this small but explosive peace talk.

The Arabs, Palestinians and Israelis who gathered in Copenhagen discovered the need to look inward, as individuals, as cultures, to see exactly what is coming from the self-creative source. They discovered what we knew: this is divinity, longing to transform the fear-based infrastructure and celebrate the diversity of its being.

After this meeting, seven Israeli school girls were gunned down by a passionate young Arab man. Certainly we were daunted, but we knew the power of our own perseverance. We knew the secrets of compassion, and the commitment to forgiveness. We keep on working, forgiving ourselves and each other as we go. To do anything otherwise will destroy the infrastructure of love we are trying to create.

Yes, the world will achieve world peace, whatever it takes, however long it takes. No matter how many journeys from spirit to flesh and back to spirit again are needed before humans willfully come to create peace, it will happen because it's the destiny of divinity.

Meanwhile, keep yourselves awake to your own musings. Listen to your own hearts, for any signs of fear or destruction. Answer those cries with compassion and non-judgment, first for your own self and then for every other human on the planet. You are the Family of Humanity, born of one tribe, possessing one soul, living on one planet, the planet Heaven on Earth.

Listen, and remember.

Manifest Destiny of
WORLD PEACE

We, the below-listed Party of Twelve, as introduced by John F. Kennedy, Jr. and scribed by Barbara With, acknowledge that our infinite spirit has been gifted with the creative life force of both humanity and divinity. We wish to now stand and state our full intention to commit world peace. We invite all inhabitants of Earth to join with us in this declaration of a Manifest Destiny of World Peace.

We intend to create into physical form a family of humankind residing on Earth who see past the illusions of the infrastructure of fear, and, through conscious commitment to self-love, self-responsibility and compassion intend to transform that fear-based infrastructure to a love-based one.

With our human and divine minds and hearts, and our physical bodies, we commit to creating peace on Earth, starting in our own center of gravity by staking a claim of complete self-responsibility to every particle of energy we put forth. From this commitment to inner peace, we intend to bring peace to every level of creation that is within our own jurisdiction.

We commit to peace within relationships between husband and wife, parent and child, master and servant, neighbor and neighbor, tribe and tribe, with our own selves. We commit to infuse each and every relationship, individual and collective, with projections of our own inner self-love with the intent to create a love-based infrastructure within those relationships.

We agree to accept responsibility for every decision that we make, for all of our personal power, and commit to use that power to enlighten, educate and inspire others to also look inward and commit to peace.

We believe that it is our destiny to manifest this peace, and that because it is destiny, there will be no obstacle or challenge too great that might prevent the actualization of this destiny. We commit to using all the elements of every challenge, no matter how destructive in nature they appear to be, to regenerate love.

We agree that all generations that have come before and all that will come after have peace as their birthright, not as an award to be earned, but a grace granted by the truth of our spiritual essence. We intend to work for the future generations, so that they may be born into a love-based infrastructure.

Lastly, we fully intend to persist with this inner movement until peace is achieved on a global level.

We, the undersigned, agree this 17th day of September, 1998, Madeline Island, Wisconsin, United States of America, Planet Earth.

Diana Spencer	Gianni Versace
Nicole Brown Simpson	John F. Kennedy
Jacqueline Onassis	Albert Einstein
Adolph Hitler	Ryan White
Norma Jean Baker	Sigmund Freud
Anwar al-Sadat	Jesus of Nazareth
John Kennedy Jr.	Barbara Lee With

_____

(Your name)

EPILOGUE

Twenty years ago today, Anwar Sadat, Jimmy Carter and Menacham Begin were concluding their historic peace talks at Camp David. As I sit here concluding my last interview, and transcribing the words of the Manifest Destiny of World Peace, I am overwhelmed by the idea that these twelve people have come together in afterlife to continue to work for peace in today's world. I am particularly honored that they have asked me to help them hatch such a brilliant idea.

Adolph brought us a chilling illustration of the more dire of possibilities of human creation. Jesus brought us a road map for changing fear to love. Diana and Gianni served the ordinary people of the world in a royal way, while Ryan White inspired us to gratitude.

Einstein knew more than a human should, and Norma Jean and Sigmund told us the secrets of sexuality. Jackie and Jack called forth dignity and grace, Anwar, courage and perseverance.

But the one who personally touched me most was Nicole. Here she sat in a group with a scientist, a movie star, a psychiatrist, world leaders, royalty, youth; an ordinary woman made famous because she had been brutally murdered. All throughout the interviews, I wondered how she would hold up in the company of these prestigious people.

Today, September 17th, 1998, on the shores of Lake Superior, I understand why she is here. She was the victim of a hideous evil. In her ordinary way, like Adolph, she is teaching the world about forgiveness.

So what will it take to get us all to look inside of ourselves and take responsibility for the fear that we project? I'm not sure. All I know is, if I don't do it for myself, no one else will do it for me.

Sounds like the perfect place to start.

Order Form
BOOKS, TAPES AND MUSIC
by Barbara With

Party of TWELVE:
THE AFTERLIFE INTERVIEWS $19.99

Diaries of a PSYCHIC SORORITY:
TALKING WITH THE ANGELS $18.95

Out of My Mind
TAPE SERIES: .... $24.99 each
Three tapes per series, channeled dissertations:
HOW TO TALK TO THE ANGELS
CHANNELING YOUR OWN DIVINITY
MANIFESTATION
PERSONAL EMPOWERMENT
REGENERATION AND PHYSICAL HEALING

Original Music .... $15.00 each
INNOCENT FUTURE: Original Soundtrack to "Diaries"
SOLITAIRE: Original solo inspirational tracks

Toll free charge orders
800-431-1579
Check or money order:
including $5 shipping for the first item/$1.50
each additional item to:

Mad Island Communications LLC
P.O. Box 22142
Robbinsdale, MN 55422

Visit www.barbarawith.com for appearances,
performances and more information.